STRATEGY

# Strategy

**A guide to marketing for senior executives**

Martin Christopher, Simon Majaro,
Malcolm McDonald

WILDWOOD HOUSE

First published in hardback 1987 by
Gower Publishing Company Limited, as *Strategy Search, a guide to marketing for
chief executives and directors.*

This paperback edition published in 1989 by
Wildwood House Limited,
Gower House,
Croft Road,
Aldershot,
Hants GU11 3HR,
England

Gower Publishing Company,
Old Post Road,
Brookfield,
Vermont 05036,
U.S.A.

**British Library Cataloguing in Publication Data**

Christopher, Martin
    Strategy, a guide to marketing for senior
    executives.
    1. Marketing
    I. Title    II. Majaro, Simon    III. MacDonald,
    Malcolm
    658.8    HF5415

ISBN 0-7045-0618-1

Printed and bound in Great Britain at
The Camelot Press Ltd, Southampton

# Contents

# Preface

Contemporary management is frequently criticized for its limited vision, for its concentration on the short term rather than the long term. Like all generalizations this view disregards the fact that the best companies today are actually run by strategists of the highest order. However, it is also true that these excellent companies are still the exception.

Our purpose in compiling this book was to share some of the lessons we have learnt from working with some of the best, and some of the less good, management teams in Europe and around the world. Our observations and those of other commentators on the management scene led us to the conclusion that there are some basic principles upon which strategic success can be based.

The focus in this book is primarily, but not entirely, a marketing focus. This reflects our own view that success in any field can only be based upon the satisfaction of customer needs. Our definition of marketing nevertheless goes beyond the traditional notion of seeking to satisfy identified customer needs. We recognize that successful strategies are always based upon the most careful analysis of corporate resources. Thus the search for strategy begins within the business in the analysis of corporate strengths and weaknesses and then progresses to the market-place in pursuit of identified opportunities.

In this book we are concerned mainly with concepts and ideas; only briefly do we examine the relevant techniques that might aid the strategist. We have included in a separate section under the heading 'Executive Action' several exercises which may help you to put these into practice. For those who wish to pursue these techniques further we have appended a select bibliography of key references.

Martin Christopher
Simon Majaro
Malcolm McDonald

# Part I
# CONCEPTS AND TECHNIQUES

# 1 The need for strategy

This book is about strategy. More specifically it is about how competitive advantage in the market-place can be gained through the use of strategy. As a concept, strategy is well understood, yet in practice truly strategic thinking is rare. Most of what passes for strategy is short term, opportunistic and reactive. The ability to take the longer view, to identify and marshall resources, and to utilize those resources in a way which anticipates market and competitor reactions, is a skill infrequently encountered.

Many commentators have sought to explain the success of the Japanese in world markets, and whilst there are as many reasons advanced as there are books and articles on the subject, one constant factor seems to emerge: strategy. It is probably not coincidental that, at the same time, a whole new industry has developed in the field of strategic consulting. For the potential client the choice of sources of advice and help is extensive, 'strategy boutiques' are as common as fast-food outlets it sometimes appears.

Perhaps because of this, something of a mystique has grown up around the idea of strategy. Even the word itself has become overworked; analyse any article in any management publication and note how often it appears. In this book we use the word 'strategy' to signify a very simple concept: using resources in a way that will gain lasting competitive advantage. Strategy is about winning over the longer term; it thus requires the confidence and discipline to plan beyond today.

It is perhaps this need to take the longer view that provides the biggest hurdle to strategic thinking. There are many pressures on every business to produce results now, not tomorrow. The stock market, the banks and risk-averse managers have all been held up in turn as the cause of this problem. What is certain is that the overwhelming concern with this year's financial results, and in particular the so-called 'bottom line', has caused, and is still causing, the decline of large parts of British industry.

The sad story of EMI and the Body Scanner provides a classic example of short-term thinking which led to disaster. The company was first in the world with a highly innovative scanner and yet failed to invest in its longer-term future, instead preferring to reap the early rewards. Competitors were not slow to enter the field with next generation machines, but rather than ploughing back cash into R&D to maintain its lead, the company 'milked' the product. In 1978 EMI's profits slumped, yet the company maintained its dividend whilst reducing still further its expenditure on R&D. The following year, close to collapse, EMI was taken over by Thorn.

It would be comforting to think of such short-term thinking as the exception. However, we encounter examples of similar blinkered thinking almost every day. Innovation, in products, in technologies and in markets, requires time and money to produce rewards. The paradox is that because the organization may not feel able to commit resources to innovation due to short-term financial constraints, the result is a greatly reduced chance of long-term survival.

It has been suggested that if there is a predominant focus in the boardrooms of the UK it is a *financial* focus rather than a *marketing* focus. The background and training of many so-called 'captains of industry' is in accountancy and finance rather than in marketing. This may account for the growth of 'paper entrepreneurialism', in which business seems to be concerned more with price–earnings ratios than with capturing markets. It is manifested also in the takeover and merger mania that has broken out once again in the recent past, where mistakenly it is assumed that acquisition can be substituted for innovation.

This, then, is the theme of the book: to suggest a means whereby the business may look beyond today to develop a sustainable competitive advantage for tomorrow.

## The strategy development process

Many models have been proposed for guiding the determination of marketing strategy. However, whilst there are numerous differences between them, the similarities are substantial.

It is generally recognized that the key to success in strategic planning is in the development of a practical process for taking an agreed statement of objectives and converting that into effective actions. In this book we will take as our framework a logic which begins with a statement of corporate 'mission' which addresses the

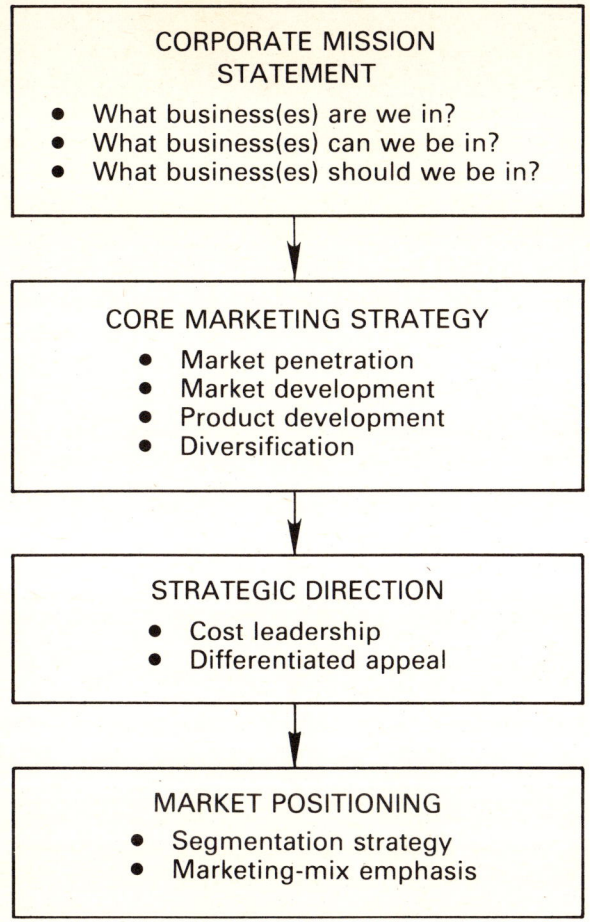

**Figure 1.1   The strategic planning process**

question, 'Where do we want to be?', and then looks at those options which are consonant with the company's strengths and weaknesses.

The choice of available marketing options will be determined not only by this definition of mission and the appraisal of corporate strengths and weaknesses but also by the company's choice of strategic direction; that is, where should we *position* ourselves? Viewed very simply, this process might be summarized as in Figure 1.1.

Each of these components of the marketing strategy process shown in Figure 1.1 is explored in detail in later chapters, but it is worth considering briefly some of the issues that are raised at each step in this sequence.

1   *Corporate mission statement*   To answer the question 'What business are we in?' requires more than just a creative imagination. Satisfactory definitions of mission must be based upon detailed analysis of the strengths and weaknesses of the business and the market opportunities that match them. Ultimately the test is not just the attractiveness of a particular business sector but the company's ability to compete within it.

2   *Core marketing strategy*   'Concentration is the key to success' may be an old marketing adage, but it still holds true. Ultimately the company will be constrained in its search for marketing success either by its knowledge and strength within existing markets or by its skills and competences with existing products or technologies. Whilst the company may venture into new markets but retain its technology/product base or seek to offer new technologies/products to existing markets, we will suggest that it is folly to move in both directions concurrently.

3   *Strategic direction*   A theme that will be pursued later in this chapter is that success in the market-place can only come from one or other of a combination of two strategic directions. These directions are cost leadership and a differentiated appeal. Cost leadership means quite simply that by one method or another we achieve a cost advantage over competitors. A differentiated appeal means that we do things differently – we 'add value' in the eyes of the customer.

4   *Market positioning*   A basic component of the strategic process in marketing is the identification of an appropriate competitive 'position' in the market-place. In essence the position of a brand or offering is simply the customer's perception of the similarity or dissimilarity of our brand in relation to competitive offerings. As such it will be influenced by the particular marketing mix of product features, promotional appeals, price level and place (distribution) that the company selects.

Whilst it is not the intention of this book to suggest that frameworks such as that described above can provide a 'formula' for successful marketing, our experience is that the successful companies are typically those that have thought long and hard about each of the four steps outlined above.

# The concept of 'mission'

We have already stressed that the process of strategy formulation has as its objective the optimum allocation of corporate resources over time. In operational marketing management terms this involves decisions, first, on which products should be offered to which markets (i.e. product/market strategy) and, second, on the specific marketing mix to be used.

However, before such decisions can sensibly be made, some preparatory steps must be taken. In particular there should be available a clearly defined statement of *corporate mission*, specifically answering the questions:

- What business(es) are we in?
- What business(es) can we be in?
- What business(es) should we be in?

Seemingly these are simple questions to answer. In reality it is a complex and difficult task to formulate a clear statement of mission which adequately summarizes the focus and direction of the enterprise. Yet without such a statement of purpose the development of viable strategies is constrained from the start.

So often, too, when these questions are raised the answers given tend to be product-focused. In other words, the business is defined in terms of the products that it makes rather than the market needs that its offerings are intended to satisfy. It is vital that the business recognizes that products (or services) are only vehicles for the satisfaction of underlying needs. Products come and go with increasing frequency and yet the underlying need structure tends to change little. The importance of this distinction between products and needs can be illustrated by reference to a successful producer of slide rules in the 1950s. This company made a range of slide rules for different applications and prided itself on the precision of the instruments and the quality of manufacture. They saw themselves as a manufacturer of slide rules and thus their business definition, had they had one, would have been couched in similar terms. Twenty years later the slide rule had all but disappeared with the arrival of the low-cost pocket-sized electronic calculator.

The message here is very clear: products have life-cycles, which means that ultimately they will die, and yet the underlying market need still remains – in this case the need for aiding personal computation.

How then should the company in this example have defined its business? It would be easy to say something like 'the provision of means for aiding computation' or similar. However, what does such a statement mean? Should the company have been prepared to move into calculators or personal computers as these technologies emerged? Clearly such strategic moves would not have been viable if the company had no strengths in those technologies.

Definition of the business must therefore extend beyond a statement of the needs that are served but must also encompass a recognition of the limited asset base of the business. In other words, the statement of mission must reflect the *distinctive competence* of the business.

In seeking to produce a corporate mission statement in any business, it is worth bearing the following points in mind. A mission statement should:

- be specific enough to have an impact upon the behaviour of individuals throughout the business
- be focused more on customer-need satisfaction than upon products or services
- reflect the distinctive competences of the business and be based upon an objective recognition of the company's strengths and weaknesses
- recognize the opportunities and threats in the competitive environment, trends in resource and consumption markets and the company's vulnerabilities
- be realistic and attainable
- be flexible.

The requirement for flexibility is of particular importance. The slavish adherence to a mission statement, even though the market environment has changed since the mission was defined, is clearly dysfunctional. Indeed it can be argued that the real value of the mission statement lies in the effort that goes into its definition and the insights that are gained through attempting to make explicit the direction of the enterprise.

But perhaps the most important of the six aspects of the mission statement as listed above is the need to recognize the limitations of the company's strengths and specifically to focus attention upon the exploitation of its asset base.

## The company's marketing assets

The textbook definitions of marketing have emphasized the satisfaction of identified customer needs as a fundamental article of faith. Various interpretations exist, but the concept of 'putting the customer at the centre of the business' summarizes these viewpoints.

Philosophically there is little to argue with in this notion. However, it must be recognized that the ability of the business to produce offerings that meet real needs will generally be limited to very specific areas. More particularly, what we find is that an organization's skills and resources are the limiting factor determining its ability to meet market-place needs. The example we quoted earlier of a slide rule manufacturer being unable to compete in the age of electronic calculators, underlines this point. The strengths and skills of that company, whatever they may have been, were quite definitely not in the manufacture of electronic calculators, whereas they may well have had a strength in marketing and distribution in specialized markets – thus possibly providing an opportunity to distribute other manufacturers' products aimed at those markets.

What we are in effect saying is that marketing should really be seen as the process of achieving *the most effective deployment of the firm's assets* to achieve overall corporate objectives. By assets in this context we refer specifically to those assets which might best be described as 'marketing assets'.

What are marketing assets? Typically when we talk about assets we think first of financial assets, or more precisely those assets that are recognized in the balance sheet of the business. So fixed assets, such as plant and machinery, and current assets, such as inventory or cash, would be typical of this view of assets.

In fact the marketing assets of the business are of far greater importance to the long-run health of the business and yet paradoxically would not appear in the balance sheet. Ultimately the only assets that have value are those that contribute directly or indirectly to profitable sales, now or in the future. Included in our categorization of marketing assets would be such things as:

- *Brand name*   What is the strength of the image or the 'values' that are created in the market place by the brand name (e.g. Schweppes or IBM)?
- *Market 'franchise'*   Are there certain parts of the market that we can call our own? The loyalty of customers and distributors will be a factor here.
- *Distribution network*   Do we have established channels of distribution which enable us to bring products or services to the market in a cost-effective way?

- *Market share*   The 'experience effect' and economies of scale mean that for many companies there are substantial advantages to being big. For example, costs will be lower and visibility in the market-place will be higher.
- *Supplier relationships*   The ability to have access to raw materials, low-cost components, and so on, can be of substantial advantage. Additionally, close co-operation with suppliers can frequently lead to innovative product developments.
- *Customer relations*   'Close to the customer' has become the motto of the 1980s, and many organizations can testify to the advantage of strong bonds between the company and its customers.
- *Technology base*   Does the company have any unique skills, processes or know-how strengths that can provide a basis for product/market exploitation?

It is only through the effective use of these and any other marketing assets that the company can build successful marketing strategies. There still, of course, remains the crucial task of seeking market-place opportunities for the exploitation of this asset base; this is an issue to which we shall return.

However, if we are to be serious about marketing assets, perhaps managerially we should treat them as we do 'financial' assets. In which case questions such as these arise:

- How do we value market assets?
- How do we protect them?
- How do we grow them?

The question of the valuation of marketing assets is complex and controversial. Traditionally the only time that an attempt is made to put a financial value on these intangible assets is when a company is bought or sold. It will often be the case that one company, in acquiring another, will pay more than the 'book value' of the acquired company – as represented, that is, in the balance sheet. The accountants' answer to this is to treat the difference between the purchase price and the book value as 'goodwill' and then to write it off against reserves or amortize it through the profit-and-loss account over a number of years. Take the case of British American Cosmetics, until recently part of the BAT empire, and the owner of many international brands such as Yardley, Germaine Monteil, and so on. When Beechams acquired the business the purchase price reflected the value of these brands, even though they were supposedly 'intangible'.

It might be argued, therefore, that if it is possible to value a company for sale, then surely it should be possible to do so on an on-going basis and specifically to recognize the worth of marketing assets.

The question of asset protection and development is in a sense what marketing is all about. The 'stewardship' of marketing assets is a key responsibility which is recognized in many companies by, for example, the organizational concept of brand management. Here an executive is given the responsibility for a brand or brands and acts as the product 'champion', competing internally for resources and externally for market position. It is but a short step from this organizational concept to a system of 'brand accounting' which would seek to identify the net present value of a brand based upon the prospect of future cash in-flows compared with outgoings.

One advantage of such an approach is that it forces the manager to acknowledge that money spent on developing the market position of a brand is in fact an investment which is made in order to generate future benefits. There is a strong argument for suggesting that, for internal decision-making and on questions of resource allocation, a 'shadow' set of management accounts be used, not the traditional approach whereby marketing costs are expensed in the period in which they are incurred but an approach which recognizes such expenditures as investments.

## The brand as an asset

First, it should be stressed that when in these discussions we refer to a 'brand' we use this term to encompass not only consumer products but the offering of any business. In some cases the company's name becomes the brand, for example IBM.

Second, a distinction should be drawn between a 'brand' and a 'commodity'. Commodity markets typically are characterized by the lack of perceived differentiation by customers between competing offerings. In other words, one product offering in a particular category is much like another. Products like milk or potatoes come to mind or tin and iron ore. Whilst there may be quality differences the suggestion is that, within a given specification, this bottle of milk is just the same as that bottle of milk.

In situations such as these one finds that purchase decisions tend to be taken on the basis of price or availability, and not on the basis of the brand or the manufacturer's name. Thus one could argue that the purchase of petrol falls into the commodity category, and whilst the petrol companies do try and promote 'image', they inevitably end up relying upon promotions such as wine glasses and games to try to generate repeat purchase.

There are examples, however, of taking a commodity and making it a brand. Take, for example, Perrier Water: the contents are naturally occurring spring water which, whilst it has certain distinctive characteristics, at the end of the day is still spring water. Yet through packaging and, more particularly, promotion, an international brand has been created with high brand loyalty and consequently it sells for a price well in excess of the costs of the ingredients.

Conversely one can also find examples of once strong brands which have been allowed to decay and in effect become commodities. This process is often brought about because the marketing asset base has been allowed to erode – perhaps through price cutting or through a lack of attention to product improvement in the face of competition. One market where this has happened in the UK is in the fruit-squash drink market. Fifteen or twenty years ago there were a number of very strong brands – Suncrush, Kia-ora, Jaffa Juice to name a few. In this market the quality of the brand had traditionally been stressed, but a switch in promotional emphasis occurred in the 1960s towards promotional offers of one

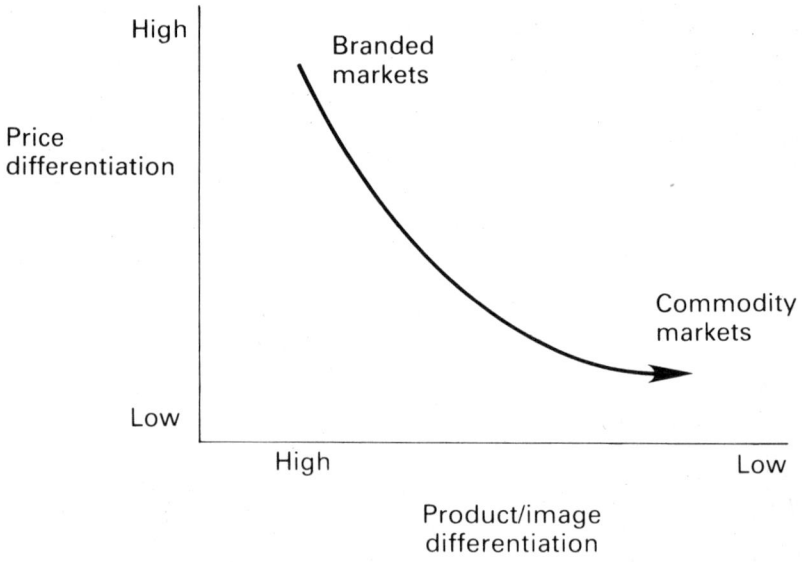

**Figure 1.2   From brand to commodity**

sort or another. Price-cutting became prevalent and resources were switched out of advertising which promoted the *values* of the brand and into so-called 'below the line' promotional activities. The main effect of this, twenty years later, has been to reduce the bottle of orange squash to the level of a commodity to such an extent that the major brands are now retailers' own-label products.

Figure 1.2 depicts the process of decay from brand to commodity as over time the distinctive values of the brand become less clear and thus the opportunity to demand a premium price reduces. So today we find a bottle of Perrier Water selling at a premium over a bottle of orange squash!

The difference between a brand and a commodity can be summed up in the phrase 'added values'. A brand is more than just the sum of its component parts. It embodies, for the purchaser or user, additional attributes which, whilst they might be considered by some to be 'intangible', they are still very real. To illustrate the power of these added values consider the results of a recent *blind* test (i.e. where the brand identity is concealed) in which Diet Pepsi was compared against Diet Coke by a panel of consumers:

- Prefer Pepsi        51%
- Prefer Coke         44%
- Equal/can't say      5%

When the same two drinks were given to a matched sample in an *open test* (i.e. the true identity of the brands was revealed) the following results were produced:

- Prefer Pepsi        23%
- Prefer Coke         65%
- Equal/can't say     12%

How can this be explained if not in terms of the added values that are aroused in the minds of consumers when they see the familiar Coke logo and pack?

The same phenomenon is encountered in industrial marketing too. In a commodity market such as fertilizers the initials 'ICI' printed on a plastic sack have the effect of communicating to the purchaser a statement about quality and reliability, giving ICI a considerable advantage over lesser-known brands.

Often these added values are emotional values which customers might find difficult to articulate. These values are given to a product quite simply through the marketing mix of product, packaging, promotion, price and distribution. All of these elements of the mix can be used to develop a distinctive *position* in the customers' mental map of the market. The concept of 'positioning' is developed in greater detail in Chapter 6, but suffice it to say at this juncture that in commodity markets competing products, because they are undifferentiated, are seen by the customer as occupying virtually identical positions and thus to all intents and purposes are substitutable. The more distinctive a *brand* position, however, the less likelihood that a customer will accept a substitute.

It is thus the case that the most effective dimensions of competition are the relative added values of competing brands. The 'core' product is purely the tangible features of the offering – usually easy to imitate. The added values that augment the product are where distinctive differences can be created. Figure 1.3 makes this point.

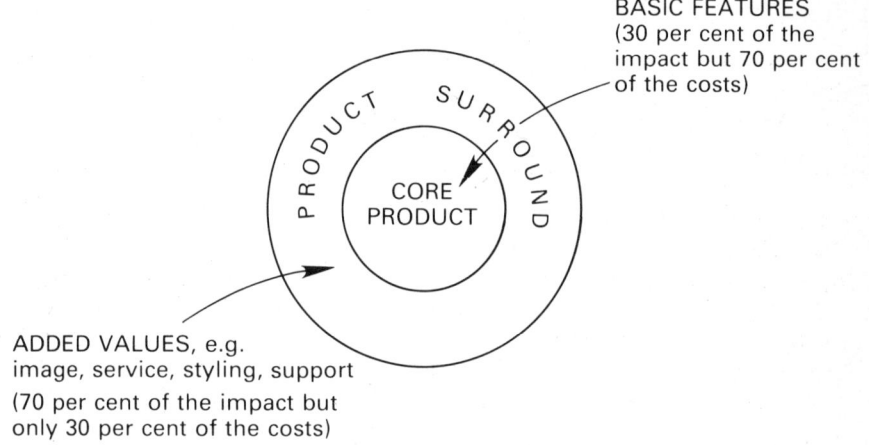

BASIC FEATURES
(30 per cent of the
impact but 70 per cent
of the costs)

ADDED VALUES, e.g.
image, service, styling, support
(70 per cent of the impact but
only 30 per cent of the costs)

**Figure 1.3   The importance of added values**

The larger the 'surround' in relation to the core product, the more likely it is that the offering will be strongly differentiated from the competition – and *vice versa*.

## The example of the British motorcycle industry

Since early this century until the 1960s the UK was a major force on the international scene in the manufacture and sale of motorbikes. Famous names like BSA, Norton and Triumph produced bikes that were sought after by enthusiasts around the world. Now, in the late

1980s, there is not a single British motorbike manufacturer left (excluding the occasional small-scale start-up operation, which unfortunately tend to be short-lived).

What happened to cause this catastrophic decline? Many words have been written on this subject, but perhaps the most detailed analysis was provided by the report prepared for the UK government by the Boston Consulting Group: 'Strategy Alternatives for the British Motorcycle Industry'. This report was commissioned in the face of the impending collapse of the last remnant of the industry.

The early 1960s saw the entry of the Japanese into the UK market. Names like Honda, Yamaha, Kawasaki and Suzuki, which were hitherto unknown in Britain, began to establish a limited toe-hold in the market. The entry strategy of companies like Honda was not to attack the established British manufacturers head-on but was initially to go for segments which were not well served. Specifically they offered models in the smallest engine categories (e.g. 125cc and under); their bikes were lightweight and easy for the inexperienced rider to handle. They incorporated innovative features such as automatic clutches and electric starters – and they were cheap.

A key part of the entry strategy was to put a major effort behind building a dealer network and in ensuring a high level of availability and product support – areas in which the British companies were notoriously weak. This entry strategy was hugely successful with a whole new generation of bike buyers. The Japanese were aiming initially not at the established motorbike enthusiasts but instead at a niche that could best be described as 'first-time buyers'. To support this market entry substantial advertising expenditure was committed and a new image of the motorbike was projected in contrast to the innately conservative approach of the established manufacturers.

From this first base in the small-bike niche, the Japanese quickly moved into the next engine size category (i.e. 250cc) again with innovative design and strong marketing support. As well as bringing with them customers who were 'trading up' from the smaller machines, they rapidly attracted sales from previous purchasers of British machines. In a short space of time the Japanese dominated this segment and before long the next category of 500cc engines.

Interestingly, the response of the British manufacturers was lethargic to say the least. It seemed as if they never really believed that the Japanese would succeed. Instead they seemed to think that they could rely upon their established position to see them through. In fact what was happening was a process of retreat as the Japanese, taking a highly targeted approach, attacked one segment after another.

In the end the last bastion, the 'superbikes' of 500cc and beyond, fell to the Japanese and with it the last of the British motorbike industry. The whole process from first entry to total domination took the Japanese a little over ten years.

What can we learn from this experience? First, the decline of the British motorbike industry and the success of the Japanese underlines in the strongest way the need for strategy. Honda, Yamaha and the others had a clear strategy; the British acted as if they had never heard of the word. The strategy adopted by the Japanese recognized the importance of selecting market segments and directing resources at those segments so that volume could be established quickly. It is not true, as many apologists for the British like to say, that the Japanese sold their machines below cost (i.e. they 'dumped' them). From the start the Japanese companies consistently made profits. The Boston Consulting Group report clearly identified the cost advantage enjoyed by the Japanese, who recognized the importance of the 'experience curve'.

Second, there is a lesson for us all in the way in which product innovation can generate a substantial value advantage. Like so many other Japanese products their motorbikes had design and technical features that gave them a high appeal in the market. Even as early as 1960 Honda had an R&D department with 700 designers and engineers which rapidly grew to 1,300 in the mid-1970s. In 1974 the remaining British company, Norton Villiers Triumph, could never muster more than a hundred engineers and draughtsmen in total.

The combination of the segment-by-segment approach in which market-share dominance was quickly achieved, bringing with it a relative cost advantage, and a strategy of innovation which gave a strong value-advantage, proved to be unbeatable.

In hindsight it all seems so obvious. However, obvious though it may be in retrospect, it should be recognized that to move into a strategic mode from a position where the short-term dominates is never easy.

The remainder of this book is aimed at providing the tools to create a truly strategic orientation.

# Overview

For too long, organizations have planned for the future mainly on the basis of the past. Planning has been a matter of extrapolation, with the focus firmly on the financial side of a company's operations.

In this chapter, strategic planning is described as long-term resource management which must not be dominated by past experience, but must instead be forward-looking, dynamic and marketing-driven.

Strategy development ideally follows a clear logic comprising four key elements:

- mission
- core marketing strategy
- strategic direction
- marketing position.

The mission, or purpose, of a company should be defined not in terms of products created but in terms of market needs, reflecting the distinctive competence of the business. Most importantly, the company must recognize its strengths and weaknesses and the value of its marketing assets.

A company's marketing assets include such things as brand name, market 'franchise', distribution network, market share, supplier relationships, customer relations and technology base. These need to be protected, developed and deployed effectively to achieve overall corporate objectives.

An example is given of the British motorcycle industry and how it fell to the Japanese, who came into the market armed with the vital ingredient the British lacked – strategy.

# 2 The search for competitive advantage

The previous chapter emphasized the concept of the 'marketing asset'. The strategic role of marketing, it is contended here, is to seek out market opportunities that will ensure the greatest return on the company's asset base. The search for appropriate strategies requires careful analysis of customers, competitors, market characteristics and environmental trends.

Figure 2.1 indicates the relationship of this analysis to the identification of market opportunities and we shall briefly consider each of the four components of this analysis in turn.

## Market analysis

Markets can be examined from a variety of viewpoints, but there are certain key dimensions that must be measured, for example:

- *Size (value, volume)* Not always easy to identify; either the data may not exist or problems arise with regard to definition – that is, what is the 'market' that we serve. This latter point is important as frequently we find we compete on a wider front for share of market. For example, a document courier service does not just compete with other couriers but with facsimile transmission as well.
- *Growth* The annual growth rate of the market, past history and future projection. In Chapter 5 we discuss the concept of the product life-cycle in detail; here we are also concerned with the life-cycle of the market.
- *Diversity* Is the market served by few or many offerings? Is it not just one market but many? How fragmented has it become? Many markets are gradually breaking up into smaller and smaller niches (e.g. fashion retailing).

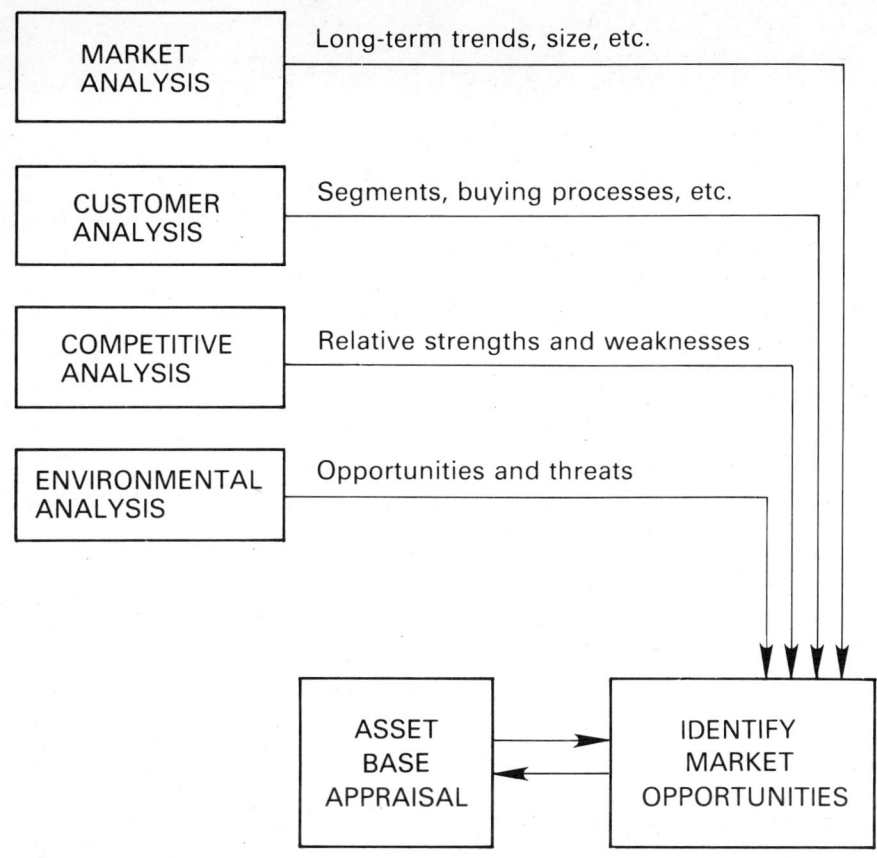

**Figure 2.1   The search for market opportunities**

- *Channels*   What is the upstream and downstream channel of distribution and supply? Where does the relative power lie? What is the strength of buyers and the strength of customers? Where do we stand in the value-added chain?

## Customer analysis

It is imperative at as early a stage as possible to stop thinking of markets in terms of numbers but instead to look at customer characteristics, whether they be individuals or organizations. The following items suggest some priorities for analysis:

- *Segmentation*   Most markets can be further subdivided into smaller sectors based upon differences between customers

either by their characteristics or by the way they respond to
marketing stimuli. We examine the concept of market
segmentation in more detail in Chapter 6; clearly it is crucial
to understand the dynamics not only of the total market but of
its component segments.

- *Buyer behaviour*  Who are the customers and who are the
  consumers? What are the important buying criteria? Who
  makes the decisions? What are the primary motivations for
  purchase? What are the principal benefits sought from the
  product? Understanding how customers buy is the key to
  successful marketing.

- *Sensitivity*  In developing the eventual marketing mix it will
  be necessary to understand the sensitivity of customers to the
  individual elements of the mix. Thus, how does the market
  react to price, to promotion, to service, to product quality,
  and so on. Such information can only come from research and
  experimentation.

## Competitive analysis

As markets decline, as growth rates stabilize or markets enter
recession, the only way to grow a business faster than the growth of
the market is at the expense of the competition. This implies a need
to understand in the greatest possible detail the competitive context
and the characteristics of specific competitors. Here the work of
Michael Porter, a Harvard Business School professor, is particularly
valuable in providing a framework for the systematic exploration of
the competitive context. Figure 2.2 summarizes the main forces
driving industry competition.

The key determinants of competitive position are:

- *Market competition*  Obviously the more numerous, or
  equally balanced, the competitors the more intense will be the
  rivalry within the market. If this is combined with a slow
  industry growth rate, and if fixed costs relative to variable
  costs are high, then the prognosis is for a high level of
  aggressive competition probably accompanied by severe price
  cutting. A further influencing factor will be the extent to
  which the competing products on offer are seen as substitutes
  by the market-place with few switching penalties for buyers.

  Of key importance will be the relative cost-structures of the
  major players in the market; these will be determined not just

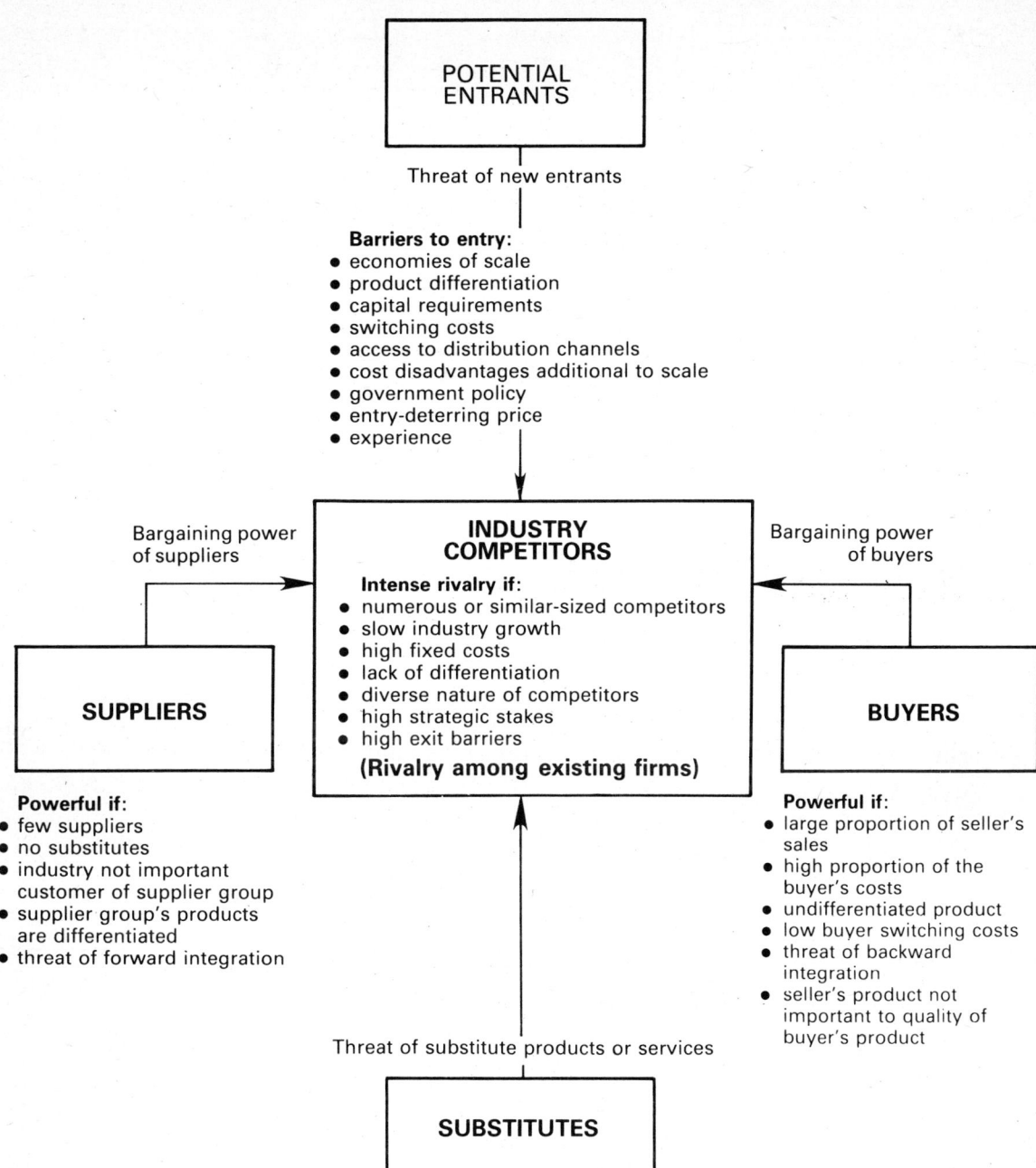

**Figure 2.2 Forces driving industry competition** (*Source*: Michael E Porter, *Competitive Strategy*, Free Press, 1980)

by market share but by capacity utilization and production technology.

- *Threats of new entrants*   In analysing markets one of the factors to be appraised is the existence, or absence, of 'barriers to entry'. In other words, how easy is it for new entrants to enter the market. Typically barriers might be provided by economies of scale so that without a minimum market share unit costs will be uncompetitive. Similarly, heavy start-up costs, whether through the need for capital investment or high levels of marketing expenditure, can provide a barrier. Government regulation, as for example in the telecommunications industry, might also prove an effective barrier.

  Conversely markets may be easy for new competitors to enter where product differentiation is low or where technology changes can overcome cost barriers. In the latter case a good example would be the way in which new technology has made it possible for new daily papers to be launched in an industry which previously had high entry barriers.

- *Substitute products*   One factor that can considerably alter the strategic balance in a market-place is the development of products that meet underlying customer needs more cost-effectively than existing products. The development of synthetic fibres had a major impact upon the demand for natural fibres for example. Similarly the advent of home video recording through video cameras has virtually eliminated the demand for home movie products.

- *Bargaining power of buyers*   The competitive climate of a market will clearly be influenced by the extent to which customers wield power through purchasing strength. Thus a market that is dominated by a limited number of buyers or where a buyer takes a large proportion of the seller's output will limit substantially the seller's opportunities for individual action or development. The UK grocery market illustrates this situation well with a handful of major retail chains being able to exert considerable influence over manufacturing suppliers' marketing policies and thus their profitability. Another source of competitive threat from buyers will occur when opportunities exist for backward integration up the value chain by buyers.

- *Bargaining power of suppliers*   Many of the threats that potentially exist from buyers can also come from the suppliers to an industry. If the supply of critical materials is controlled by a few suppliers, or if an individual company's purchases from a supplier constitute only a small part of his output, then freedom of manoeuvre may be limited. Again, if opportunities exist for forward integration by suppliers, a further source of potential competitive pressure will exist.

Competitive analysis at this level requires access to a wide range of information, necessitating a continued monitoring of all sources of data. Ideally a 'data bank' should be established on the competitive environment; use should be made of annual reports, annual statutory returns, Dun & Bradstreet reports or their equivalent, trade-press and financial reports, publications from trade associations as well as company catalogues and advertisements.

Information can often be gathered from customers and suppliers about competitors' actions or intentions. If personnel are recruited from competitors, they should be 'debriefed' as far as professional ethics allow. In fact frequently it is surprising to see just how much competitive intelligence can be gathered by making use of the sources described above, all of which are openly available.

# Environmental analysis

The marketing environment in which the company competes is wider than its customers and its competitors. Government, the economy, society and technology are all variables outside the control of the business, yet all are capable of substantially effecting the viability of the firm's marketing strategy.

- *Government* The legislative and regulatory framework within which the firm operates effects most marketing decisions either directly or indirectly. Price controls, quality standards, advertising standards, competition policy all to a greater or lesser extent will effect the ability of the business to manoeuvre. Equally, many companies have found that the legislative environment can provide opportunities. Companies making tyres clearly benefited from the UK government's decision to tighten up on the minimum tread depth for cars on the road, for example.
- *The economy* Every business will have linkages, directly or indirectly, with the broader macro-economy. Interest rates impact on costs but also on the customer's ability to buy; exchange rate fluctuations have similar consequences. Infla-

tion, unemployment, taxation, capital allowances, and so on, are an ever-present part of the macroeconomic environment and all must be factored into the strategic thinking of the firm.

It is not surprising that economic forecasting and analysis is a growth industry with more and more companies recognizing that one of the major factors influencing success or failure – the economy – whilst entirely outside of their control, must still be monitored.

- *Society*  Business in the Western world has come to recognize the growing importance of societal issues in the market-place. Consumer movements have shown that when issues arise that generate public concern their ability to change corporate strategy can be considerable. Ecology, pollution, quality of life are increasingly important issues to be explicitly taken into account in the development of the firm's strategy. Once more, however, it should be emphasized that these changes in the environment can bring about as many opportunities as they do threats.

- *Technology*  The impact of technology change upon marketing strategy has already been commented upon. The increasing rate of change in many industries is leading to shorter product life-cycles and higher risks of failure. The advent of microprocessors is a prime example of a technology step-change that had a major effect not only on the computer industry but on many other industries too. To compound this market turmoil the microprocessor has itself experienced technological change several times in its brief life.

It has become a cliché to point to the need for technology monitoring and forecasting within the context of marketing planning – yet it is vital. Of equal importance to the anticipation of technology change is the ability of the business to be flexible in its strategic response. If technology changes then so too must our strategy.

## The dimensions of strategy

Of late, substantial interest has been shown in the sources of competitive advantage. In other words, what is it that makes one particular company a success in the market-place whilst others struggle to keep up? *In Search of Excellence* became a bestseller on the basis of its exploration of this theme, and other investigations have been widely reported. Although there can never be complete agreement on such a complex and dynamic process, it would appear that there are two predominant dimensions of success.

Put very simply, successful companies either have a productivity advantage or they have a 'value' advantage or a combination of the two. The productivity advantage gives a lower-cost profile and the value advantage gives the product or offering a differential 'plus' over competitive offerings. Let us briefly examine these two vectors of strategic direction.

## Productivity advantage

In many industries there will typically be one competitor who will be the low-cost producer and, more often than not, that competitor will have the greatest sales volume in the sector. There is substantial evidence to suggest that 'big is beautiful' when it comes to cost advantage. This is partly due to economies of scale which enable fixed costs to be spread over a greater output but more particularly to the impact of the 'experience curve'.

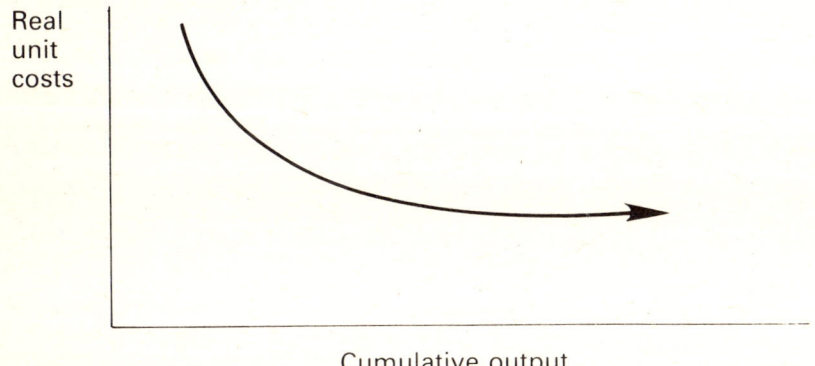

**Figure 2.3   The experience curve**

The experience curve is a phenomenon which has its roots in the earlier notion of the 'learning curve'. Researchers discovered during the Second World War that it was possible to identify and predict improvements in the rate of output of workers as they became more skilled in the processes and tasks on which they were working. Subsequent work by Bruce Henderson, founder of the Boston Consulting Group, extended this concept by demonstrating that *all* costs, not just production costs, would decline at a given rate as volume increased. In fact, to be precise, the relationship that the experience curve describes is between *real* unit costs and *cumulative* volume. Further, it is generally recognized that this cost decline applies only to 'value added', that is costs other than bought-in supplies.

The experience curve in its general form is shown in Figure 2.3. There are many implications of this relationship for the development of marketing strategy, not least in the determination of pricing strategy. However, its importance in this current discussion is in the fact that if one company's relative market share is greater than its competitors, then, other things being equal, it should be further down the experience curve. In other words, it will have a cost advantage. Such a cost advantage can either be used to lower price, thus putting the squeeze on competitors, or higher margins can be earned at the same price as competitors.

Later in this book it will be suggested that it will generally be preferable to use such a cost advantage to reinvest in the product rather than use it to initiate price wars and thus run the risk of reducing the product to the status of a 'commodity'.

## Value advantage

It has long been an axiom in marketing that 'customers don't buy products, they buy benefits'. Put another way, the product is purchased not for itself but for the promise of what it will 'deliver'. These benefits may be intangible; that is, they relate not to specific product features but rather to such things as image or reputation. Alternatively the delivered offering may be seen to outperform its rivals in some functional aspect.

As we explained in Chapter 1, unless the product or service we offer can be distinguished in some way from its competitors there is a strong likelihood that the market place will view it as a 'commodity' and so the sale will tend to go to the cheapest supplier. Thus the importance of seeking to attach additional values to our offering to mark it out from the competition.

What are the means by which such value differentiation may be gained? Essentially the development of a strategy based upon additional values will normally require a more segmented approach to the market. When a company scrutinizes markets closely it frequently finds that there are distinct 'value segments'. In other words, different groups of customers within the total market attach different importance to different benefits. Benefit segmentation is discussed in greater detail in Chapter 6, but its importance here lies in the fact that often there are substantial opportunities for creating differentiated appeals for specific segments. Take the motor car as an example. A model such as the Ford Sierra is not only positioned in the middle range of European cars but, within that broad category, specific versions are aimed at defined segments. Thus we find the basic, small engine, two-door model at one end of the spectrum and the four-wheel drive, high-performance version at the other extreme. In between are a whole variety of options each of which seeks to satisfy the needs of quite different 'benefit segments'. Adding value through differentiation is a powerful means of achieving a defensible advantage in the market.

In practice what we find is that the successful companies will often seek to achieve a position based upon *both* a productivity advantage *and* a value advantage. A useful way of examining the available options is to present them as a simple matrix as in Figure 2.4.

**Figure 2.4   Strategic direction**

Let us consider each of the options in Figure 2.4. For companies who find themselves in the bottom left-hand corner of our matrix the world is an uncomfortable place. Their products are indistinguishable from their competitors' offerings and they have no cost advantage. These are typical 'commodity' market situations and the only ultimate strategy is either to move to the right on the matrix (i.e. to cost leadership) or upwards into a 'niche'. Often the cost leadership route is simply not available. This will particularly be the case in a mature market where substantial market-share gains are difficult to achieve. New technology may sometimes provide a window of opportunity for cost reduction, but in such situations it is often the case that the same technology is available to competitors.

Cost leadership, if it is to form the basis of a viable long-term marketing strategy, should essentially be gained early in the market life-cycle. This is why market share is considered to be so important in many industries. The 'experience curve' concept, briefly described earlier (see Fig. 2.3), demonstrates the value of early market-share gains – the higher your share relative to your competitors, the lower your costs should be. This cost advantage can be used strategically to assume a position of price leader and, if appropriate, to make it impossible for higher-cost competitors to survive. Alternatively price may be maintained enabling above-average profit to be earned, which is available to further develop the position of the product in the market, if so desired.

The other way out of the 'commodity' quadrant of our matrix is to seek a niche or segment, where it is possible to meet the needs of customers through offering additional values. Sometimes it may not be through tangible product features that this value-added is generated but perhaps through service. For example, a steel stockholder who finds himself in the commodity quadrant may seek to move up to the niche quadrant by offering daily deliveries from stock, or by providing additional 'finishing' services for his basic products or by focusing upon the provision of a range of special steels for specific segments.

What does seem to be an established rule is that there is no middle ground between cost leadership and niche marketing. The relationship between size, differentiation and profitability is generally agreed to be as depicted in Figure 2.5. Being caught in the

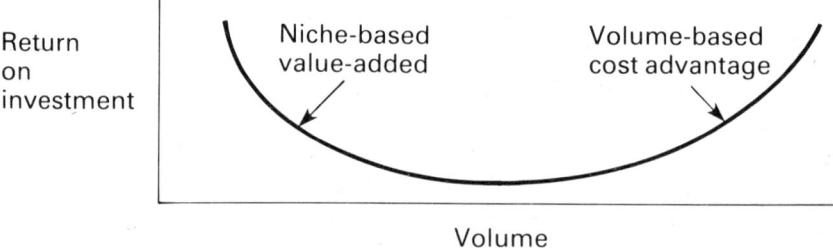

**Figure 2.5   The dangers of the middle ground**

middle – that is, neither a cost leader or a niche-based provider of added values – is generally bad news.

Finally, perhaps the most defensible position in the matrix shown in Figure 2.4 is the top right-hand corner. Companies who occupy that position have products that are distinctive in the values they offer *and* are also cost-competitive. It can be argued that many Japanese products, particularly in consumer markets, have achieved this position. Clearly it is a position of some strength, occupying 'high ground' which is extremely difficult for competitors to attack.

# Market share strategies

In discussing the advantages and disadvantages of pursuing niches or volume it is important that the issues surrounding 'market share' be fully understood. That there is a strong relationship between market share and return on investment (ROI) has been confirmed by the analysis of data from thousands of companies participating in the PIMS (Profit Impact of Market Strategy) study. This study, in searching for explanations of variations in profitability between firms, identified a strong correlation between market share and ROI.

However, a warning should be sounded: it may well be that profitable companies have high market shares, but it does not follow that all high-market-share companies will be profitable. Quite simply this is because market share can be 'bought'. It can be bought through price reductions, increased marketing effort and product development. All of this can be good practice unless it is at the expense of long-term profit. Some companies have failed to recognize that investing in market share is really only viable early on in a product/market life-cycle. Likewise other companies have been caught out when the product/market life-cycle turns out to be much shorter than was anticipated. In summary, market share strategies are long term, and in volatile markets such strategies must be pursued with care.

A further issue surrounds the question, 'Share of *which* market?'. In other words, what is market share a measure of? The answer is it all depends on how we define the total market. A holiday tour operator specializing in organizing cultural tours of sites of antiquity accompanied by a professor of archaeology is not operating in the same market as a tour operator offering ten days in Majorca for £200. Yet they both offer holidays.

The definition problem is helped if we use the concept of the 'served' market. The served market is best described in terms of the specific needs that we seek to meet rather than some generic product category. Some have called market share in this context 'share of mind', meaning that when potential customers are contemplating a purchase to meet a specific need they limit their choice to offerings that they consider competitive.

The strategic problem may thus be seen as one of how to increase 'share of mind' amongst specific target groups. Here it is worth examining the dynamics of market share and thus gain a closer insight into the determinants of share.

One contribution to our understanding of the determinants of market share is provided by Frank Lynn & Associates, the international consultants, who see market share as the product of three factors:

- product-line coverage – how much of the market our product line is aimed at
- presence or market coverage – how well our product is distributed
- hit rate – what proportion of sales opportunities are converted.

Thus it is suggested that market share can be viewed as a simple relationship:

Product-line coverage × presence × hit rate = market share

So a company with a product line that only covered 50 per cent of the market's needs and was only available in 50 per cent of the outlets and was only chosen 50 per cent of the time when compared with its competitors by customers would only achieve a 12.5 per cent market share (i.e. 50 per cent × 50 per cent × 50 per cent). Clearly, therefore, the key to market share improvement lies in the management of each of these three key variables.

A variation on this concept is shown as Figure 2.6, where it is suggested that market share should be computed on the basis of the proportion of the total *available* market, and thus our share is influenced by our product and customer coverage. Looking at market share in these terms helps explain why the definition of market share is crucial if strategies for share expansion are to be adopted. Such analysis helps explain the basis for a given market share and thus may provide guidelines for improvement.

Even allowing for these problems of definition, companies that seek to achieve cost leadership through market share may still be disappointed. The fact is that different products and processes may

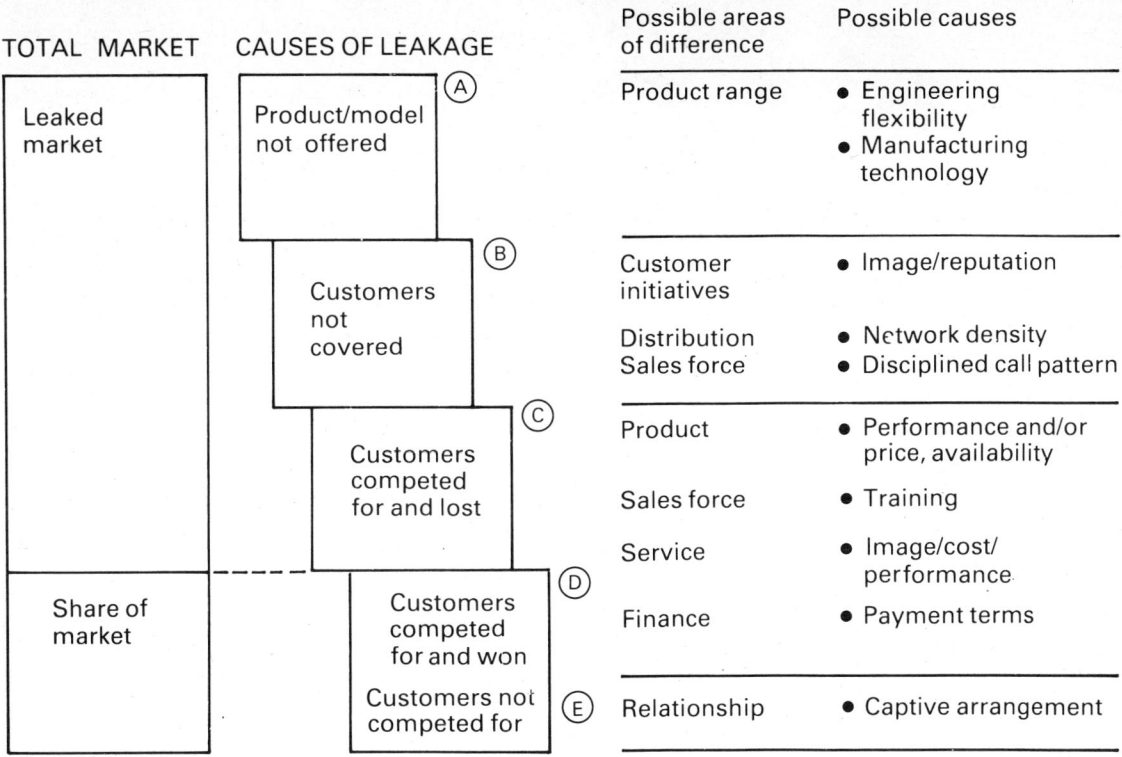

| TOTAL MARKET | CAUSES OF LEAKAGE | | Possible areas of difference | Possible causes |
|---|---|---|---|---|
| | Product/model not offered | Ⓐ | Product range | • Engineering flexibility <br> • Manufacturing technology |
| Leaked market | Customers not covered | Ⓑ | Customer initiatives | • Image/reputation |
| | | | Distribution Sales force | • Network density <br> • Disciplined call pattern |
| | Customers competed for and lost | Ⓒ | Product | • Performance and/or price, availability |
| | | | Sales force | • Training |
| | | | Service | • Image/cost/ performance |
| Share of market | Customers competed for and won | Ⓓ | Finance | • Payment terms |
| | Customers not competed for | Ⓔ | Relationship | • Captive arrangement |

*Useful definitions:*
- Share of market = D + E
- Winning ratio = D/(C + D)
- Market coverage C + D + E

**Figure 2.6   Determinants of market share** (*Source*: K. Ohmae, *The Mind of the Strategist*, Penguin Books, 1983)

have different opportunities for cost reduction. In other words, the shape of the experience curve can differ from one business or activity to another. This is particularly important when a company competes with other companies who have a greater or lesser degree of integration, backwards or forwards, in the 'value-added chain'.

The idea of the value-added chain is that at different stages of the manufacturing–marketing–distribution chain, value is added to differing degrees. Depending upon the degree of involvement (i.e. integration) in the different value-adding activities in the chain, the company may be better positioned to take advantage of experience curve effects compared with a competitor whose activity structure does not allow such opportunities.

Figure 2.7 gives an example of two companies who compete in the home-computer market. Company A is more heavily integrated 'upstream' – that is, it is involved in component manufacture – whereas Company B is more heavily integrated 'downstream', – that is, it is involved in assembly and retailing and not in component manufacture. The size of the blocks represents the proportion of total added value available at the end stage in the total value-added chain. The shaded area represents the extent to which each company is involved in that activity.

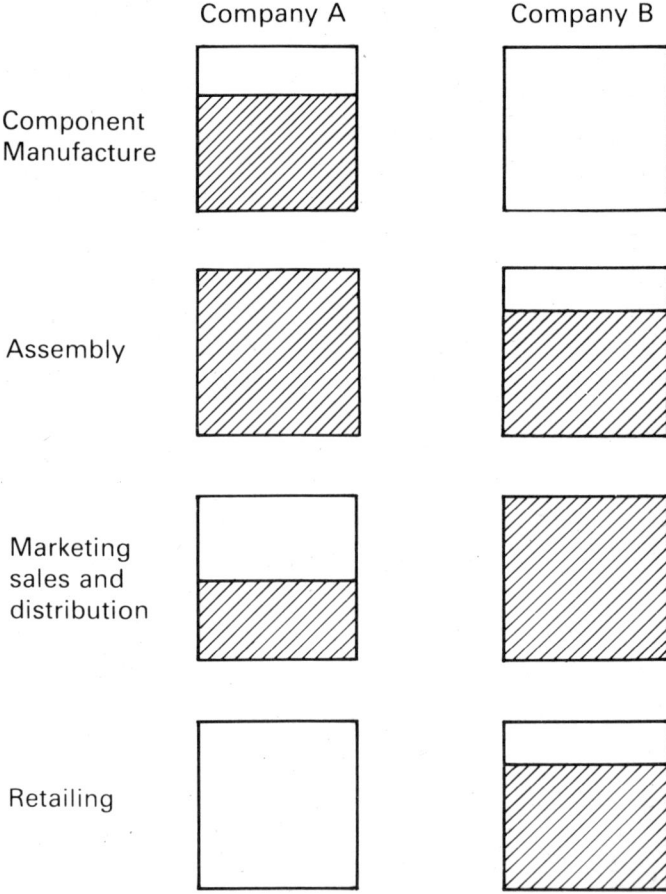

**Figure 2.7   The value-added chain**

Whilst the total value-added that each company in Figure 2.7 receives looks roughly equivalent, the opportunities for cost reduction, and hence value-added improvement, may vary considerably.

For example, if the slopes of the experience curves for each component stage of the value-added chain are different – as they surely will be – then an increase in sales volume of a certain magnitude would have a different effect on the two companies. Let us say that relevant experience curve slopes are as shown below (the 'slope' percentage indicates that after a doubling of cumulative output the real unit costs of the activity would be that percentage of their initial value):

|                               | *Slopes* |
|-------------------------------|----------|
| Component manufacture         | 85%      |
| Assembly                      | 80%      |
| Marketing, sales, distribution| 75%      |
| Retailing                     | 75%      |

Thus it would appear that Company B has a better chance of achieving a cost leadership through a market share increase as a result of his particular activity balance, that is a greater involvement in that part of the value chain where the opportunities for cost reduction through volume are greatest. Company A's opportunity for cost leadership is likewise reduced, thus indicating that a market share strategy may be less appropriate for him.

## Overview

Marketing's strategic role is to find market opportunities which will allow for the greatest return on the company's assets. This requires analysis of:

- market
- customers
- competition
- environment

Research has shown that successful companies have either productivity or value advantage in the market-place. A productivity advantage is gained when real unit costs decrease as cumulative output increases, thereby giving the company a cost advantage in the market. A value advantage occurs when different groups of customers within the total market attach different importance to different benefits. Value is thus added through differentiation and becomes a corporate strategy.

There seems to be no middle ground between cost leadership and what is described here as 'niche marketing'. Companies in the middle usually find themselves in grave trouble.

To decide whether to pursue niches or value we must understand the determinants and definitions of market share and that, most importantly, market share must result in a return on investment. Volume is not the same thing as 'profitability' because companies may find that their market share is bought at too high a cost. Therefore, market share strategies must be created for the long term, taking particular care in volatile markets.

# 3 Strategy search and creativity

Having clear corporate objectives is not a guarantee of success. However, not having such objectives is likely to cause serious problems and possible failure. It is not unlike saying to a person who takes regular and energetic exercise that such activity cannot guarantee that he will continue to enjoy good health. Yet it is probably much safer to tell the person who never takes any such exercise that his health is likely to be at risk.

The process of setting objectives has to start at the top, at the strategic level of the firm. It is totally inappropriate for middle management to embark on an objective-setting exercise in an organization in which the people at the top dissociate themselves from the all-important task of searching and reflecting upon the choice of the most appropriate and attainable objectives for the corporation.

In many companies top management attempt to delegate this task to a 'corporate planner' or some other person with an impressive title. Whatever the quality of such individuals it is important to emphasize that formalizing a set of corporate objectives and searching for suitable strategies is the job of the chief executive and his top team. One can delegate the collection and analysis of data needed for the planning process. Similarly one can delegate the task of collating and consolidating sub-plans and the management of the procedural aspects of the planning process. However, the chief executive cannot abdicate from the intellectually demanding task of codifying and communicating to every member of the organization the corporate objectives – the banner under which every person in the firm will need to plan their respective jobs and duties.

The corporate objectives are the 'tablets of stone' that top management present to the people for guidance, inspiration, confidence and faith. On the other hand, unlike the biblical tablets of stone, these 'tablets' need to be dynamic and must be updated in response to a myriad of external and internal pressures.

So far nothing that has been said is novel, none the less it is useful to explore some of the problems that many corporate strategists have to face during the strategic planning process. Failure to grapple with such problems often nullifies the many benefits of the planning process. Moreover, we shall explore how creativity can enrich the quest for a more meaningful and effective corporate strategy.

# A dynamic 'input'

'Proactive' is a popular word among planners. Being 'proactive' means anticipating the future and responding to such a vision of likely events. The planning task normally expects management to gaze at the future and endeavour to prepare a series of plans that will take the firm from present-day realities into that future. This means that one must plan in response to a probable scenario that one truly believes is likely to occur. Such belief in future events must be based on analysis, forecasting skill, judgement and creativity.

Many companies have suddenly collapsed because somewhere along the line top management has failed to gaze, effectively and intelligently, into a crystal ball and anticipate the likely events and pressures which may affect the firm's future. Too often top management is content to plan on the basis of sheer extrapolation of the past. Unfortunately, steady success in the past can breed the kind of complacency and arrogance that convinces management of the firm's invincibility in the future.

We have recently met a newsprint paper manufacturer in one of the Scandinavian countries who, during the planning process, instructs his planning officers to prepare a thirty-year futuristic document. 'Why thirty years?' we asked. The answer was most enlightening inasmuch as it showed how proactive the chief executive and his planning team are. They have recognized the fact that immense changes are likely to occur in the field of printed communication in the future. Yet it takes thirty years for trees planted today to become ripe for paper manufacturing. Thus it is essential to consider all the implications during the preparation of today's plans. It is quite easy to ignore such a distant future and simply continue to operate as they have been doing during the last fifty years.

It has been interesting to observe the broad-minded way in which this company's planners are prepared to consider and assess the many challenges which are likely to alter the firm's marketing and technological environments. Will newspapers as we know them exist in thirty years' time? Will telephone directories be printed or will people use small terminals for directory enquiries? Will the *Encyclopaedia Britannica* be available as a microchip for use on domestic personal computers? Many similar questions are being posed and reflected upon in great depth every year during the planning cycle.

All this deliberation and analysis has convinced the top management that the firm may be reaching a watershed point in its strategic direction. Hitherto they considered their business to be in the 'manufacturing and marketing of paper'. Clearly the nature of the business and its manufacturing processes have imposed upon the firm a certain degree of production-orientation. However, the threats identified, albeit not yet fully quantified, stimulated the firm's strategists to consider an alternative route into the future without affecting drastically the present operations. The following set of objectives has emerged:

- We are currently in the communication business but are based entirely on the visual-printed sector of this trade.
- In our specific segment our market share is x per cent and our objective is to maintain this level. (At this point detailed objectives are set for specific countries and markets.)
- Details of profit objectives are stated for specific products, markets and operating units.
- We forecast a strong move away from the 'printed-visual communication' system in existence into a telecommunication/audio-visual-based system where the consumption of paper will decline or change in character.
- We therefore propose to build such a perception into our corporate thinking and wish to add the following objectives to our mission:
  - We shall reduce our total dependence on wood-based paper products during the next five to ten years.
  - We propose to take steps towards broadening our activities into the communication business irrespective of the media used but at the same time seek to capitalize upon our well-established strengths and experience.
  - We shall allocate towards such a development the sum of $Y million and our aim is to make it viable in accordance with our prescribed criteria within five years.

This is a brief synopsis of a dynamic approach to the strategic planning process and the setting of objectives. The company has opened new perspectives for itself and can now start exploring alternative routes for achieving the objectives set. Obviously a host of alternative strategies such as new product development, merger, acquisitions, and so on, should be identified and screened. The important point is that a new banner for corporate reflection has been established. The firm is not content to plan for the future on the basis of a static world immune from change.

Few companies take adequate account of the external environment and its dynamism. Table 3.1 sets out some examples of external developments likely to occur in the future and affect the fortunes of companies operating in the relevant industries.

**Table 3.1**
**Future developments likely to affect companies**

| Likely developments | Impact on specific industries |
| --- | --- |
| *Changes in life-style* | |
| Consumer increased interest in own health and safety (so-called 'ME-culture') | Food industry through increased preference for health foods and avoidance of many ingredients deemed less wholesome. |
| | Sport goods industry – greater demand for products seen as particularly beneficial for the maintenance of good health. |
| | Health-care clinics and centres. |
| | Medical insurance. |
| Continued decline in work ethic | Leisure and recreation industries. |
| | 'Do-it-yourself' industry. |
| | Security industry – owing to an increased crime rate (leisure activity for some ...). |

**Table 3.1** (*continued*)

| Likely developments | Impact on specific industries |
| --- | --- |
| *Interest in the ecology* | Packaging industry – significant impact likely to occur in relation to various products which are not bio-degradable or likely to pollute the environment.<br>Energy, fuel and power industries – stronger legislation against smoke and other environmental pollutants likely to emerge and affect their plans. |
| *Demographic*<br>Decline in the nuclear family | Housebuilding and furniture industries – different size and configuration of accommodation and furnishing will probably be required in the future. |
| Ageing population in the West | Can impact on many industries such as food, housing, insurance, pensions, transport, and so on – obviously it presents an opportunity for some; a threat for others.<br>Medical services and pharmaceuticals. |
| Decline in number of children | The projections of current birth rate into the nineties onwards will inevitably have an impact upon:<br>• clothing and shoes for children<br>• anything pertaining to education<br>• the food industry. |

**Table 3.1** (*continued*)

| Likely developments | Impact on specific industries |
|---|---|
| *Technological* <br> We live in an age of enormous technological changes. It is very important that each company analyses and forecasts the impact that these changes are likely to have on its future. For example: <br>     Telecommunication, video-conferencing and electronic mail | Will probably have untold influence on the work habits of individuals in a firm, their travel requirements, office needs. This is likely to impact upon many industries associated with the provision of office equipment and services. <br> Multi-location companies like banks, building societies, supermarkets, travel companies, and so on, will undergo immense administrative changes through the availability of incredibly fast communication networks. <br> The consumer will be able to interface with banks, shops, airlines, and so on, without leaving home. An opportunity for the electronic hardware and software industries and the physical distribution business(?)! |

**Table 3.1** (*concluded*)

| Likely developments | Impact on specific industries |
| --- | --- |
| *Biotechnology* | Likely to have an enormous impact on the pharmaceutical and chemical industries and also on the whole health-care associated businesses. |
| *Political*<br>  Laws designed to conserve energy | So far only limited attention has been paid by politicians towards the need to conserve energy. Assuming that more radical laws on the subject are introduced, the impact on the following industries could be far-reaching:<br>  • transport services and car industry<br>  • domestic appliances, mainly heating<br>  • insulation and solar energy<br>  • winter clothing. |

Table 3.1 includes just a few challenging statements of threats and/or opportunities that the strategic planner has to consider with great depth and intellectual wisdom. The whole purpose of the planning process can be nullified if the future is ignored and only the past and the present provide the 'input' upon which plans are based. Insurance companies which ignore the likelihood of future changes in tax relief on life assurance and pensions clearly do so at their peril. Manufacturers of pharmaceuticals who fail to perceive the effort that governments will invest in saving money on the national drug bill live in the proverbial fools' paradise. Opticians who fail to forecast the fact that the government is determined to break the

'closed shop' attitude of the industry cannot claim to be dynamic planners.

# A need for creativity

'Creativity' is not an ingredient that one normally associates with the strategic-planning process. One often believes that creativity is only appropriate during product development, the design of promotional campaigns and similar activities. The advertising and design industries would let us believe that they are the custodians of creative ideas.

'Creativity' has a vital role to play in the strategy search process. Moreover, a genuine and wholehearted application of creative thinking to the strategic-planning process will not only enrich the future direction of the firm but will also help to stimulate an organizational climate in which creative ideas can spawn. It is always important to remember that creativity does not just happen. It has to be developed and stimulated in a relentless way with the major impetus coming from the top. Top management cannot isolate itself from creativity and exhort everybody in the organization to be more creative. The cue must come from the strategic level of the firm, and if that level is seen to think and behave in accordance with the principles of creativity, the chances of the whole company behaving in a similar way are greatly enhanced.

Surely the incorporation of creative ideas into the strategic planning cycle and the process of setting of corporate objectives, is an admirable starting point for getting the creative juices going throughout the organization and developing the kind of attitude which every innovative firm requires.

Before exploring how creativity can help in strategy search it is appropriate to define a couple of terms which often confuse managers: 'creativity' and 'innovation'. They can be defined as follows:

- 'Creativity' is the thinking process which helps us to generate ideas.
- 'Innovation' is the process of applying such ideas towards doing things in a *better* and/or *cheaper* way (and, where a tangible product is involved, innovation can occur when such a product is more *aesthetic*).

In other words, 'creativity' is the raw material; 'innovation' is the result. Invariably there is a rate of exchange between the ideas that one needs to screen before one of them deserves the privilege of implementation. Research carried out a few years ago suggested that the ratio between 'ideas' and commercially acceptable 'innovations' (as defined above) is, on average, 60 : 1! 'Ideas' are needed in quantity; 'innovations' are needed for their quality. The former could include good, mediocre and even ridiculous ideas (the so-called 'intermediate impossibles'); the latter should only permit commercially acceptable and results-orientated activities.

A number of logical corollaries emerge from what has been said:

- If one wants to innovate, one must attempt to 'catch' a large number of ideas. At the creativity stage one must not be too concerned with the quality of each idea.

- Management must be sufficiently broad-minded to be prepared to consider and ventilate 'way-out' ideas and strategies. Strategists who are afraid of thinking laterally or explore ideas which at first glance appear eccentric or impractical can starve the company of fresh and imaginative strategies.

- Linked with the previous point, it is important that top management scans the horizon for strategic ideas experimented with and tried by other firms, irrespective of the industrial and commercial sector they belong to. Strategic excellence can often be gleaned from companies operating in totally different types of business. A bank that refuses to learn from the successes demonstrated by detergent manufacturers, and the domestic appliances manufacturer who shuts his mind to novel strategies of a transport firm, are both less likely to emerge with exciting innovations in their respective plans.

- Procedures for screening ideas and retaining the practical ones and rejecting the less appropriate ones must be developed. Clearly, if one accepts the 60 : 1 ratio one is liable to be smothered by ideas. It is important that a filtering process supported by criteria of relevance and commercial validity is developed.

- Finally it is appropriate to state that creativity calls for managerial courage and a certain amount of venturesome attitude. It is unlikely that a fainthearted top management will have sufficient pluck to consider truly creative avenues for future exploitation. Conservatism and lack of imagination often dampens the planners' enthusiasm for a strategy which might deflect the firm from its well-trodden course. Unfortunately this happens quite frequently even in situations in which obvious warning signals of future dangers have been identified.

As ordinary citizens we frequently observe how some industries and companies appear to be heading straight for a turbulent future without taking steps to avoid the squalls which even a casual observer can detect on the horizon. Sometimes it is almost inexplicable that great companies like Dunlop, which at one stage enjoyed a high reputation and a worthwhile market share in many of their activities, got themselves into such a sorry state. It is not unfair to assume that, in addition to all its managerial weaknesses, a fundamental lack of creativity existed at the top during the process of searching for fresh strategic directions.

We read in the financial press about the serious problems that Midland Bank has had as a result of the large losses incurred by Crocker Bank, until recently its US subsidiary. Inevitably one is asking oneself a few pertinent questions such as, 'Why did Midland decide to buy an American Bank when the challenges facing all banks in the UK as a result of strong potential competition from building societies and so on are so daunting and call for so much attention, resource allocation and creativity?' Is it possible that top management chose the wrong strategic direction?

We all believe that BL's collapse at the end of the 1970s stemmed in the main from industrial relations and overmanning problems. Undoubtedly these were serious matters, but one is perfectly entitled to reflect upon the probability that the root cause was an unimaginative, uncreative and non-dynamic management. We know of enough instances of car manufacturers around the world who have managed to grapple with enormous challenges and achieve creditable levels of success. The most notable example is BMW, who managed to rise like a phoenix from the ashes of the 1960s as a result of a creative and clear-thinking re-positioning strategy.

The creative strategist analyses with care the information gathered during the audit phase of the planning cycle. He then attempts to coalesce all this input into a set of objectives supported by a cluster of appropriate strategies for achieving these objectives. Creativity in this regard means that he is not afraid of searching for a novel and sometimes unorthodox direction. A manufacturer of small diesel engines who is unable to sell his machines owing to cash-flow problems among his customers could explore the strategy of installing such machines on client premises for a peppercorn fee and in addition invoice a charge on 'units of power produced' on these machines. This is how Xerox started their meteoric success. Sometimes the idea may be impractical but may none the less contain the seed of a worthwhile strategy. The fainthearted strategist will reject it out of hand; the more venturesome one will consider it on its merits in a more constructive and innovative fashion.

Ideally one should be in the happy position of having a large number of objectives and strategies to consider and evaluate in some depth before one can commit oneself to a specific route. As explained earlier, there is no harm at this stage in looking at what may easily seem far-fetched ideas and strategies.

In this connection it is sometimes helpful to resort to a number of techniques which may help the planning team to generate a myriad of ideas for subsequent screening during the planning cycle. It is better to filter and reject ideas by the score than start with a single strategic choice based on a conservative commitment to the direction of the past. A few of these techniques will be explored briefly.

## Techniques for generating ideas during the planning cycle

The planning team may consist of a group of highly creative individuals who do not require artificial methods for enriching their imagination and mental fertility. However, it is rare to find such teams. In most companies top management is so preoccupied with the running of the business and having to deal with a host of problems that by the time they come to search for a strategy they desperately need a prod for creative thinking.

The following techniques, adapted for use during the corporate planning process, can enrich the proceedings and the quality of the output that may emerge at the end of the cycle.

### *Brainstorming*

The word 'brainstorming' is often used in a very loose form to represent a general discussion aimed at generating new ideas. In fact the word was first coined by Alex Osborn, who in the late 1930s wrote a fascinating book called *Applied Imagination*, in which he described a precise technique for solving problems through the process of collecting a large number of ideas spontaneously generated by a group of participants. Osborn defined 'brainstorming' as, 'A conference technique by which a group attempts to find a solution for a specific problem by amassing all the ideas spontaneously contributed by its members'. A few general rules normally apply to the way an effective brainstorming session is held:

- The participants in the proceedings must temporarily suspend judgement. In other words, every idea, however absurd, will be recorded for subsequent screening.
- Uninhibited thinking is desirable. The wilder the idea, the better; it is easier to tame an idea down than to 'think up'.
- Quantity is wanted: the greater the number of ideas, the greater the probability that a few of them will be really good.
- Combination and improvement is encouraged. In addition to contributing ideas of their own, participants are encouraged to suggest how the ideas of others can be combined to yield yet another idea.
- A member of the team should act as a 'scribe'. His or her task is to record all the ideas that have been put forward by the participants.

A long list of ideas should emerge from a brainstorming session, and a thorough screening and evaluation of each idea should follow. Later we shall discuss a number of aids to this screening activity.

Let us now revert to the earlier example of the company that manufactures paper out of pulped wood and the new range of objectives that it has set for itself. Their current problem is how to select a strategic route for attaining such objectives. It is all very well to define a set of objectives; it is much more difficult to know how to go about achieving them.

We could imagine that the top management has decided to resort to a short brainstorming session with the view of generating a number of ideas as to the kind of strategies which they may usefully evaluate and analyse. The group consists of seven people: five directors, the corporate planning officer and an outside management consultant who acts as the chairman of the session. His main role is to ensure that the ideas flow at a rapid rate (between 100 and 125 ideas in twenty minutes is an average output) and that all judgement is totally suspended during the session. One of the participants acts as the 'scribe' who records all the ideas that are raised.

It is important to come to terms with the fact that during a well-run brainstorming session the list of ideas may encompass a few impractical and sometimes even crazy ideas. Brand and product managers seldom flinch at the sight of such ideas. Advertising people almost love them. They all know that quite often such 'intermediate impossibles' finish as great innovations. Unfortunately in most companies the people at the top are far less tolerant of eccentricity and creative zeal, especially when they deviate from a conservative posture.

Let us now simulate the kind of output which might have emerged from a brainstorming session in the forest products company we previously described. Below we list a batch of ideas that the 'scribe' might have recorded.

- Supply the kind of paper that computer stationery manufacturers require.
- Enter the computer stationery business offering to make and print the full range of such products.
- Offer to sell the company to IBM as the 'in house' producer of their computer printout stationery.
- Buy a printers/typewriters company and offer to supply unlimited paper with every typewriter at a preferential price.
- As before but give the printers and the typewriters away free-of-charge and charge a fee on a 'per character' printed or typed (like Xerox with their photocopying machines).
- Get out of paper altogether and turn the forests into leisure complexes.
- Change the technology with the view of producing tissues and toilet paper. These are less likely to be affected by the telecommunication revolution.
- Concentrate on markets and countries which are underdeveloped and are less likely for a while to abandon the 'printed word' as a communication system.
- Go downstream by publishing books, magazines, journals, and so on.
- Take over firms, like Reed International, who have developed diversified activities but yet are large consumers of paper.
- Use our profits from identified 'cash cows' in order to buy our way into the information technology industry.
- Set fire to our forests and use the ashes as fertilizers.
- Set fire to our forests and use the insurance money towards entering the 'Office of the Future' business (It hurts? You must gnash your teeth and bear it!)
- Enter the insurance business – they use a lot of paper.
- Buy a bank – they use even more paper.
- Get into plastics and manufacture credit cards, plastic money, and so on.

- Offer to print for the Open University – they use a lot of paper.
- Develop an Open University concept in countries which do not have such a system. This will get us into audio-visual communication, which also requires a lot of paper. We can kill two birds with one stone through such a strategy.
- Develop a 'Prestel' type of service which would include a printer thus allowing users to print their own paper daily. Obviously we shall supply the paper.
- And so on.

Many of these ideas may sound ridiculous, but out of 120 ideas the must be a probability that a few sensible ideas will emerge. It is the ability to stomach such esotericism that guarantees a place for creative thinking in an organization.

Later we shall see how this myriad of ideas – the good, the bad and the indifferent – can be screened and evaluated.

## Synectics

The word 'synectics', which originates from the Greek, was first applied to the field of creativity by W.J.J. Gordon, who was the co-founder, together with George Prince, of a company they named Synectics Inc. Under this title they encompassed the process of gaining new and creative insights to solving problems through bringing together elements that are diverse in character and normally unrelated.

The approach developed by Gordon and Prince became a complex method for generating ideas and solving problems. In its simplest form it is an attempt to draw metaphoric analogies between a given problem and parallel situations from other spheres of discipline or even from nature.

It is inappropriate here to discuss in the detail the synectics sub-routines. For the purpose of this chapter, suffice it to say that the aim of synectics is to search for solutions by casting one's attention to other activities in our world, however remote they may appear at first glance, and explore the way they managed to grapple with analogous problems. Thus, if the question is how to improve the camouflage of military vehicles, we can invite the zoologist to tell us all about camouflage in the world of animals. An understanding of the way the chameleon changes his colours and other animals place themselves in various backgrounds to hide themselves from sight can be a fertile source of ideas for development.

In the context of strategic planning this method could be applied in a modified way. The planning team could simply seek to list comparable situations that have occurred in different industries and try to learn from the solutions that such companies have evolved in response to similar problems. Again the secret lies in not being afraid of exploring and discussing ideas emanating from remote environments and disciplines.

The following examples illustrate how a number of companies developed creative strategies as a result of a synectics-type approach:

*Casa Homes Ltd*

During a very sluggish economic period following the oil crisis a housebuilder found it exceedingly difficult to sell his new houses. The firm's objectives were to sell around 120 units per month. At that point of time the sales dropped to less than one half of that figure. It needed no imagination to realize that the company would soon get into serious trouble.

After much heart-searching the management came to the conclusion that the main reason for the consumer resistance was the general feeling of uncertainty that made potential customers worried about committing themselves to a house purchase in a specific location. The situation was further exacerbated by the fact that house prices at the time were depressed.

'What will happen if I am forced to move as a result of a job change? How easily could I sell my house in such circumstances?' This was fear that the firm sought to alleviate. It felt that if it could manage to solve this problem it would become easier to achieve the sales objectives set.

In a synectics-type session the group sought to identify how other companies, organizations or individuals have managed to deal with such a situation. These were a few of the ideas that were ventilated at that session:

- Car dealers offer a second-hand price based on the Glass directory. Alternatively they take the old car in part exchange.
- The John Lewis Partnership claims as part of its marketing communication that they are 'never knowingly undersold'.
- Most holiday bookings cannot be cancelled within a certain period from departure date. The consumer is invited to insure himself against the risk of unavoidable cancellation.

At this point the team explored at some length whether a similar arrangement could be developed when a sudden need to sell a house for unavoidable reasons occurs.

- A few large travel agents guarantee money refund in the event that the tour operators become bankrupt.
- The managing director suddenly remembered that when he went to a West End gallery the salesman offered to give him, in writing, an undertaking that should he wish to sell the picture at any time in the future the gallery would buy it from him at the price he had paid in the first place.

This idea triggered the imagination of those present and before long it emerged into a promotional strategy: all house buyers were offered a 'buy-back' certificate in the event that circumstances forced them to have to sell the house in a hurry.

The idea was developed and implemented and proved most effective. In other words, 'creativity' was turned into a successful 'innovation' in terms of the definition propounded earlier. The inspiration for this idea came from a synectics-type metaphorical analogy exercise.

*Alemap Stationers Ltd*

This firm owned many retail outlets selling stationery and office equipment. The overall performance of the firm was poor and this was mainly due to the fact that the only profitable outlets were the 20 per cent of the shops that generated 80 per cent of the sales.

The objectives of the firm were stated as follows:

- to survive
- to remain in the office consumables business
- to supply 'hardware' office equipment only to the extent that it might help subsequently to sell consumables (the 'derived demand' approach)
- to attain certain figures of sales, profits and ROI – all specified.

The obvious strategy in support of these objectives was to look at each shop in turn and close down or sell all those shops that did not meet certain standards of performance. Unfortunately a reduction in the number of shops would cause a decline in sales and this in turn would reduce the purchasing power of the firm as a whole with a resultant increase in product costs. This was the dilemma in a nutshell.

A synectics group was assembled with the task of identifying alternative strategies through drawing 'metaphorical analogies' with other industries or other activities in human endeavour.

Many ideas emerged and were considered. The main ones were as follows:

- McDonalds run their business as a cluster of franchise deals, yet they supply all the raw materials, thus enjoying a large purchasing power.
- Coca Cola give a licence to 'bottlers' who have to adhere fully to a large range of conditions and guidelines plus buy the concentrates from Coca Cola.
- Holiday Inn group is a cluster of franchises with strong conditions attached thereto.
- Abbey National Building Society and other societies use estate agents as sub-branches.
- The Post Office use small haberdashery shops, grocers and general stores as sub-post offices.
- Boots the Chemists often sell stationery, maybe Alemap should start selling toiletries and medicines?
- In the US, 'drive-in' banks are quite popular – maybe we could have 'drive-in' stationery shops?
- On the subject of franchise one encounters an increasing number of successful operations in the clothing business such as Benetton, 'Tie-rack', and so on, who run a rapidly growing chain of franchise-holdings. Can this represent an idea for strategic exploration.

These are just a few metaphorical analogies that a synectics session can highlight. Many others can be identified and each one deserves a long enough discussion with the view:

- to depart from a narrow and sometimes myopic strategic perspective to which planners often find themselves committed
- to derive ideas and creative inspiration from other spheres of activity and businesses
- to develop fresh strategies for evaluation.

In practice 'brainstorming' and 'synectics' are fairly similar in their objectives and approach. Some of the complexities that have been ascribed to them in the literature have only managed to frighten managers from making use of them and especially in the case of 'synectics'.

The main difference between the two techniques is that in the case of 'synectics' one is trying to indulge in creative extrapolation from other spheres of human endeavour or even from the nature around us. As a result the most successful 'synectics' sessions occur when one brings into the proceedings people with diverse disciplines, such as zoology, psychology, biology, architecture, and so on. The synergy of a multidiscipline group can enrich the process of generating a large number of fruitful and imaginative 'metaphorical analogies' out of which at least a small number can represent real winners.

Many modifications and embellishments of the last two techniques have been developed during the last few years. They carry fancy names like 'recorded round robin', 'wildest idea', 'intermediate impossible analysis'. It will be outside the scope of this book to explore them in detail. Nevertheless, it is important to remember that the process of searching for the most appropriate strategic route for a firm calls for as much creativity as any other area of management. It is therefore not inappropriate for top management to spend some time getting acquainted with the whole subject and making use of the techniques which one has discovered as the most useful.

## Morphological analysis

Once again this is a simple technique which was allowed to become complex through the enthusiasm of overzealous advocates. The result has been that the average manager is deterred from using it or experimenting with it.

The main aim of this technique is to single out the most important dimensions of specific problems and then examine all the relationships among them. 'Morphology' means structure, and the technique seeks to explore all the possible 'sub-structures' that a multidimensional matrix yields.

The best way to illustrate the use of the technique and its appropriateness to strategic planning is through a short case study:

Tactile Packaging Ltd is operating in the immensely competitive packaging field. As part of the strategic planning cycle the firm has decided that it is vital for it to explore the development of new concepts in packaging as well as the development of new markets for existing products. It has become clear to top management that the chance of survival with the present range of products is grim.

As part of the marketing planning task it has decided to look for many products/markets ideas. A three-dimensional matrix was assembled. On one axis a large number of alternative shapes were listed (e.g. cube, sphere, tube, cone, etc.). On the second axis all possible products that need packing were shown (e.g. milk, smells, powders, etc.), and on the third axis the materials or combination of materials from which the packs could be made were added. The outcome, as shown in Figure 3.1, consisted of 7 × 7 × 9 = 441 ideas.

The company's strategists were convinced that among the 441 ideas thus generated there were bound to be a few excellent ideas which might help to change the fortunes of the organization.

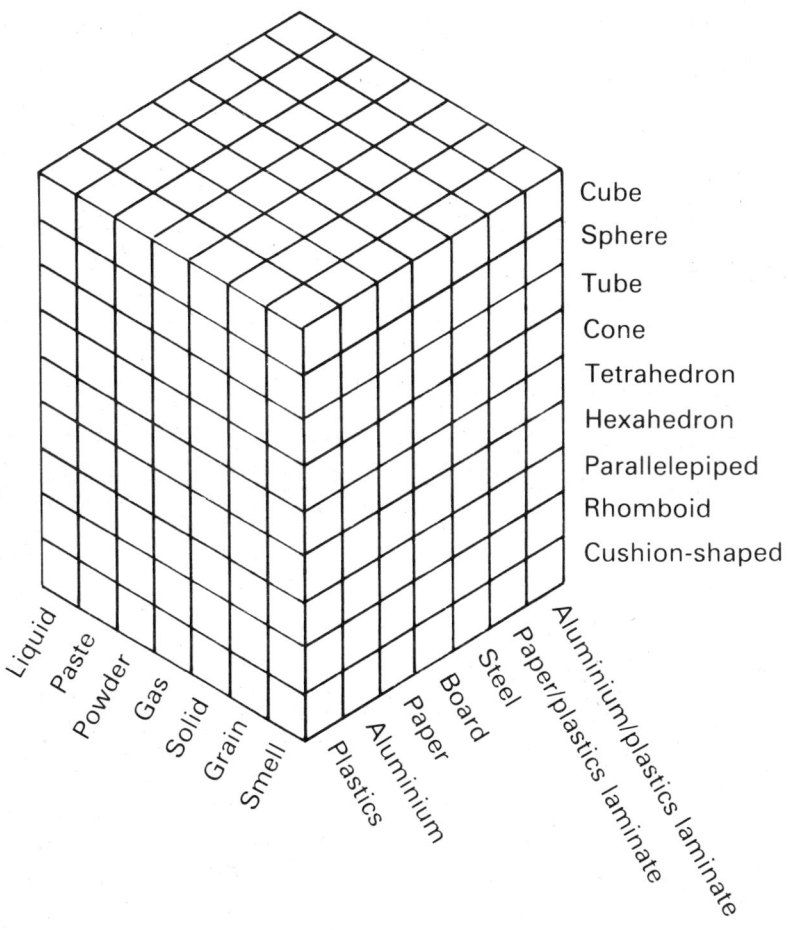

**Figure 3.1   Morphological analysis**

This kind of analysis does not always solve firms' problems. Nevertheless, the mere process of taking a lateral leap can help the planners to break away from the routine cycle of a repetitive and turgid planning process.

Morphological analysis is particularly helpful when a company has reached a certain level of stagnation and it desperately needs to open new strategic vistas for the future. Thus a company that derives most of its profits and cash flow from tobacco will wish to identify a number of industries and/or activities towards which to direct its strategic thinking. Clearly such activities must be compatible both with the firm's specific strengths as defined during the SWOT analysis and also with the 'opportunities' that the econometric, socioeconomic and technological scenarios appear to indicate for the future.

# Evaluating ideas

One of the problems associated with creativity is the fact that one often lands oneself with a vast number of ideas and it is quite easy not to know how to cope with this multitude. As emphasized earlier, every idea deserves suitable attention until the contrary is proved. The temptation is to short-circuit the process and reject ideas fairly ruthlessly in order to save time. Unfortunately among the ideas thus rejected may be one or more that really deserve careful exploration.

In the context of strategic reflection centred around top management it is important that clearly laid-out procedures are developed in order to facilitate the evaluation of strategy ideas. The existence of such procedures can facilitate the delegation of the evaluation task to less senior members of the strategy search team.

No hard-and-fast rule exists as to what an appropriate set of procedures should encompass in this regard. However, it is desirable for such procedures to meet the following characteristics:

- They must be flexible in approach. It would be most regrettable if the procedures that one establishes for assessing and evaluating creative ideas are so rigid that the whole process of innovation is stifled as a result.
- Clear commercial and technical criteria of acceptability must be available during the initial screening and feasibility stages of the evaluation. The filtering process must be capable of examining the merits of ideas however exotic they may appear at first glance. It is therefore vital that the evaluators have at

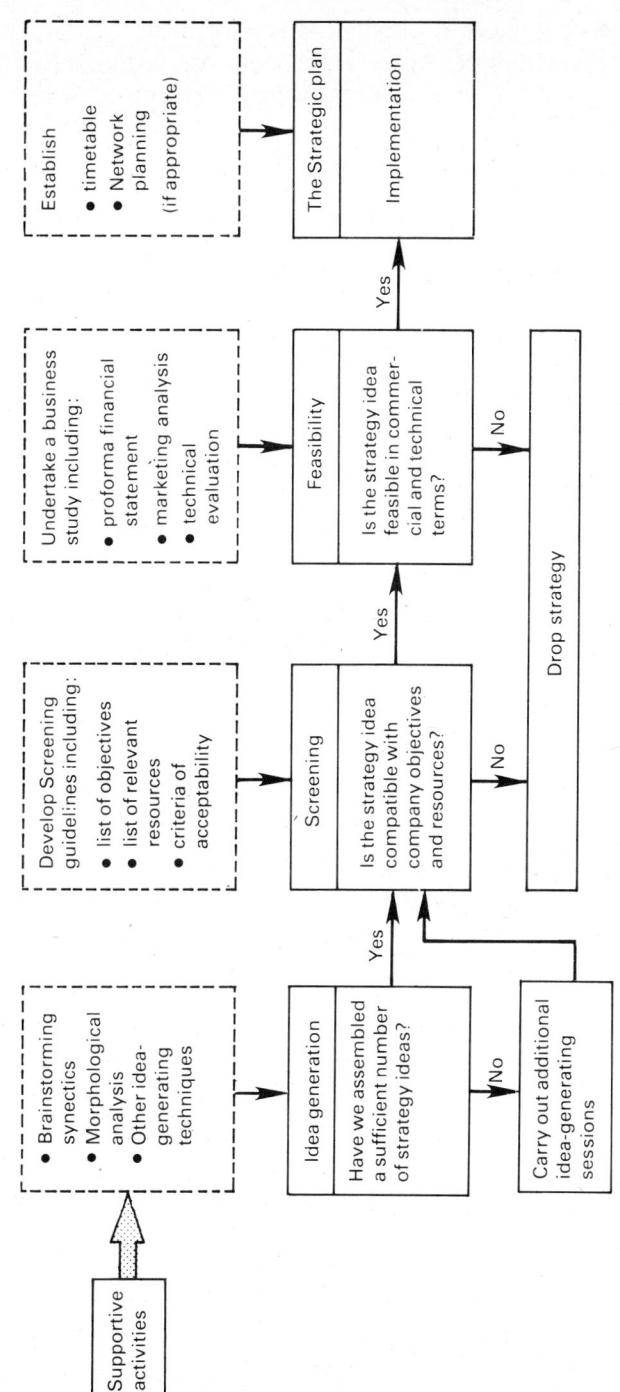

**Figure 3.2  A framework for evaluation procedures**

their disposal a list of objectives and resources against which the compatibility of each idea can be examined.

Figure 3.2 provides a conceptual framework for an evaluation system showing the interrelated steps which need to be undertaken coupled with the various supportive activities that effective procedures should include.

## Overview

Setting clear corporate objectives does not guarantee success, but it certainly increases its probability. However, to be useful, objectives must be set at the most senior level in the organization. It is not a task to be delegated, although certain aspects of implementation can be assigned down the line.

A key ingredient of corporate strategy is described here as 'proactivity'. This means that the strategy must be flexible enough to respond to external and internal environments, while retaining its core sense of direction.

Creativity is another vital ingredient of the strategic planning process. This, too, must emanate from the top echelon of the organization and be encouraged throughout. It is the fresh influence of the creative spirit which keeps organizations aware and responsive.

A distinction is made between creativity and innovation, to demonstrate the usefulness of each. Creativity is the 'thinking' stage of an idea's generation, while innovation is what makes the idea work. Therefore, organizations should search for ideas in quantity but apply qualitative thinking to innovation. By allowing ideas to surge in, organizations can promote their generation and even permit unorthodox notions to be developed.

Various techniques for generating ideas are discussed in some detail: brainstorming, synectics and morphological analysis.

Ultimately, ideas must be evaluated. The temptation to reject ideas too quickly must be resisted, and instead a clear process, identifying criteria within a framework of flexibility, must be established.

# 4 Strategic positioning and segmentation

Market segmentation is not a new concept. It has formed an important part of the curriculum ever since the whole subject of marketing became an integral part of management development. Indeed, it is rare to find a course, a seminar or a workshop on marketing which does not encompass a number of sessions on 'market segmentation' and concepts allied to it.

However, there has been a strong tendency to discuss the subject in the context of marketing management and marketing operations rather than within the framework of corporate strategy and long-range planning. The result has been that in many organizations the concept is well-understood by marketing personnel only and the initiative for exploring segmentation strategies rests in the hands of those responsible for planning marketing activities. The result is that in those companies in which marketing management is weak the probability of identifying and exploiting creative and profitable market segments is greatly diminished. It is very unlikely in such companies that other functions such as manufacturing, R&D or finance would be in the position of pursuing the conceptual discipline of identifying and measuring market niches towards which the company should target its effort.

It is important to remember that whilst 'market segmentation' is essentially an integral part of marketing strategy, the impact on the firm's fortunes can be so far-reaching that top management would not be performing its strategic function if it were to dissociate itself from the detailed process of evaluating segmentation policies. Abdicating from such a process may simply mean that the ultimate decision whether to position the company and its products in specific segments, as against catering for everybody in the market-place, rests in the hands of the marketing department only. Clearly such decisions must be explored from the vantage point of top management, and the impact on other functions must be carefully assessed.

In the light of these remarks it is intended to consider the whole subject from a strategic viewpoint rather than from the more limited and parochial marketing perspective.

## The strategic reason for segmenting markets

Every firm needs to ask itself once in a while a few fundamental questions:

- Are we able or willing to satisfy the needs of *everybody* in the market-place?
- Bearing in mind our specific strengths and weaknesses, are we better off to concentrate upon one or a few segments in the market only?
- What is better for us, being a small fish in the ocean or being a large fish in a small pond?
- Are we capable of fighting the giants of our industry or are we more likely to succeed by 'positioning' ourselves in segments of the market in which our competitors are not operating?

In practice a company can only answer these questions once it has completed the dual analysis of (1) internal strengths and weaknesses and (2) external threats and opportunities. The whole essence of the SWOT analysis is to assess accurately what the company is capable of doing in a competitive environment.

Clearly, if one finds oneself competing against General Motors, one must ensure that one is not fighting such a giant in the same market arena. One must be prepared to steer clear of the markets in which the giant is enjoying considerable strength and market penetration. It is much easier to fight in a portion of the market in which General Motors are weak. Such weakness may stem from a number of reasons:

- The market segment is too small for them (but big enough for their smaller competitor).
- They have difficulties in reaching such a segment as a result of the absence of an effective distribution system.
- They simply feel that they have better opportunities for their resources elsewhere.

It is always useful to remember that what is an opportunity for Company A is not necessarily an opportunity for Company B.

The creative marketer who has limited resources at his disposal should seek to identify the 'corners' or 'gaps' or 'niches' in the market which the well-established competitors have ignored or failed to perceive. This in turn may mean that the company can develop a marketing programme which would enable it to gain a dominant position in that 'gap'. Such a strategy has a considerable commercial attraction in certain circumstances.

In the early 1960s BMW was undergoing a serious financial crisis. The company was facing enormous marketing threats from powerful competitors such as Ford, General Motors, Volkswagen and many others. The company's range was antiquated and unattractive. The management recognized that the only chance for survival depended on the ability of the firm to develop a range of new motorcars which would be readily acceptable to the market-place or to various segments in it. Moreover, they realized that whatever product strategy they might adopt must not be in a direct competitive conflict with their bigger and more powerful competitors. In other words, a decision was taken to develop a segmentation strategy whereby the firm would identify a 'gap' in the market which was either 'underpopulated' or fairly easy for them to penetrate.

We all know what an amazing recovery BMW have attained since that period. In fact today BMW is probably one of the most successful car manufacturers in the world when measured in terms of growth, return on capital employed and market share of specific segments as against the market as a whole. There is little doubt that this success stems in the main from a clear-thinking market segmentation and 'positioning' strategies.

The main creativity associated with this strategy was the actual process of analysing the competitive scene in detail and identifying 'holes' in what was available in the market-place. Knowing one's competitors in depth and understanding in which part of the market they are positioned, whether by design or by accident, is probably one of the most valuable inputs of effective marketing. It is in this connection that BMW have excelled during the strategy search period.

In seeking to analyse and understand one's market-place and the relative position of competitors, a useful creative technique called 'mapping' can be employed. The idea underlying mapping is that if one is able to identify the two or three major parameters that affect buying decisions in a heavily populated market-place, one can record the interplay between these two factors on a scatter diagram.

By the time this exercise is completed one can have a clear picture of the areas which are congested with competitive activity and those which are more sparsely populated. Sometimes one is even lucky enough to identify totally empty areas on the 'map'. Clearly such anomalies deserve thorough investigation. An empty 'hole' on the diagram does not necessarily mean that market opportunities exist. However, if subsequent consumer research does indicate that a positive marketing opportunity exists in the empty area one must actively investigate the viability of such a segment within the firm's strategic environment.

The mapping process is normally experimental and a number of combinations should be explored. One is never sure that 'gaps', 'holes' or other aberrations will result from the exercise. Nevertheless, it is a worthwhile analysis, and even where no surprises emerge it helps to ensure that a thorough understanding of the competitive ecology is gained.

In the car business one might assume that the two major factors that affect buying decisions are price and performance, or price and economy, or even cubic capacity and price. In the 1960s the likelihood was that the main elements that affected the consumer's decision were the first two parameters, namely price and performance. The important point is that any factor selected for analysis must be capable of quantification. 'Performance' is a little vague. On the other hand, 'maximum speed' is measurable, and the appropriate data can be gleaned from the manufacturers' published specifications and/or manuals.

Figure 4.1 illustrates the kind of picture which an analysis undertaken in the mid-1960s would have looked like. BMW positioned themselves in the gap shown in the centre of the figure. They not only managed to attain considerable success in that area but have also managed to achieve some dominance in the segments encompassed by that zone.

The main purpose of this brief example is to illustrate that the process of identifying and quantifying segment opportunities is not just a marketing exercise. It is much more fundamental – in many situations it can represent the difference between strategic renewal and corporate demise. To that extent the impetus for this kind of strategic exploration must be masterminded from the top and not left to functional management.

## Bases for segmenting markets

Few areas in the field of strategy search offer greater scope for creativity than the process of identifying and evaluating segmentation options. Once a firm discovers that it is not able to take the market leaders in a head-on battle, the search for segmentation and

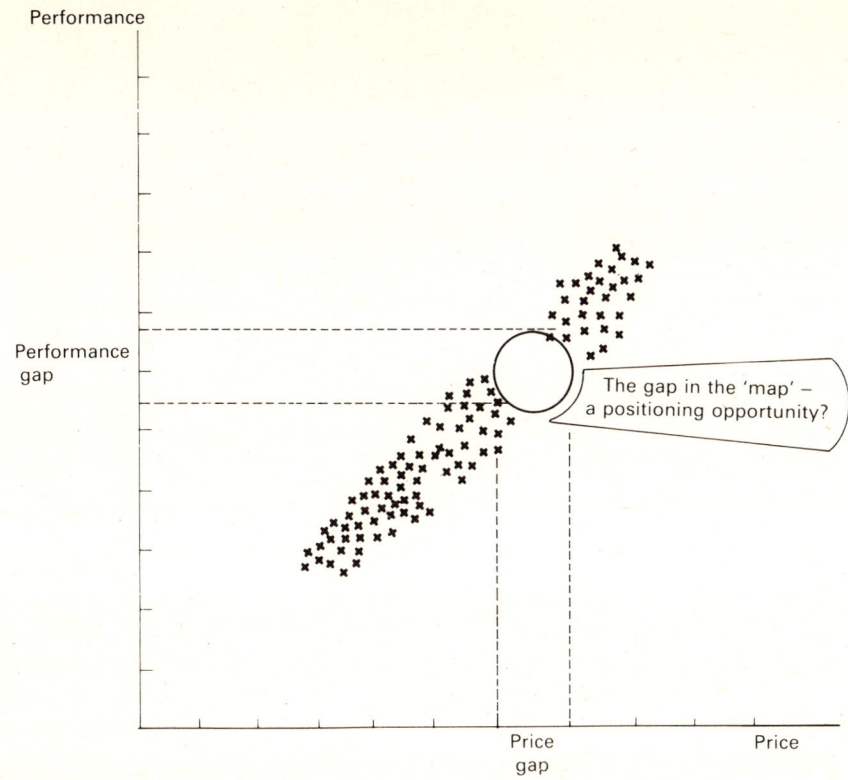

**Figure 4.1   Mapping exercise of the car marketing scene in the 1960s**

positioning alternatives becomes a vital part of the corporate planning process. Usually the firm that is able to inject maximum creativity into this activity is the one which is likely to achieve true excellence in its ultimate performance.

In this regard it is appropriate to emphasize that it is seldom the obvious segmentation choice which offers the route to success. The winning segment is often the one which has not been discerned by the main adversaries in the market-place either because it is too dynamically advanced (the 'proactive segment') or it represents an innovative way for analysing and stratifying markets.

Thus the food companies that anticipated the gradual move of an increasing number of consumers towards a healthier diet (the 'ME Culture') were able to position themselves strongly in this growing segment. They could achieve this without having to battle with the giants of the industry who were too obsessed with their market shares in an undifferentiated market-place. By the time the giants decide to enter into the 'health food' niche the early entrants were well entrenched and it is fairly difficult to dislodge them.

The choice of bases for segmenting markets is endless. It lends itself to a very vivid and fertile brainstorming exercise. Whilst a number of commercial constraints preclude the validity and acceptability of some segmentation avenues, one must be prepared to look at as many alternatives as possible during the idea-generation stage. The more segment ideas one can evaluate, the more one is likely to identify creative niches for exploitation.

As suggested earlier, identifying bases upon which markets can be segmented calls for considerable creativity and imagination. Attempting to list all the alternative options would be foolhardy. All we can do here is provide a number of typical illustrations as to how markets have been segmented in the past. The reader must recognize that the only limits to the plethora of alternatives that may exist in the real world are managerial vision and creative thinking.

The following are a few of the obvious bases upon which market segments have been identified and exploited in the past:

## Socioeconomic segments

In this connection marketers often tend to accept the well-established systems that exist in each country. In the UK we accept too readily the system that divides the households into the AB, C1, C2, D and E categories. Other systems exist in other countries. It is quite obvious that if one only looks at existing and well-proven segmentation 'infrastructures' one is liable to fall into the trap of having to fight other companies that have analysed the market in accordance with the same system and discovered the same segment opportunities.

The truly creative strategist looks for a novel basis upon which to divide the market-place. It may still be based on the socioeconomic dimension, but it may encompass an original nuance that others have failed to perceive. Whoever discovered in the USA the marketing attractiveness of the so-called 'Yuppies' segment (the 'Young Upwardly-mobile Professionals') has undoubtedly demonstrated a shrewd and highly original analytical skill. Members of this segment have proved to be not only highly homogeneous in their purchasing pattern and behaviour but have also been prepared to

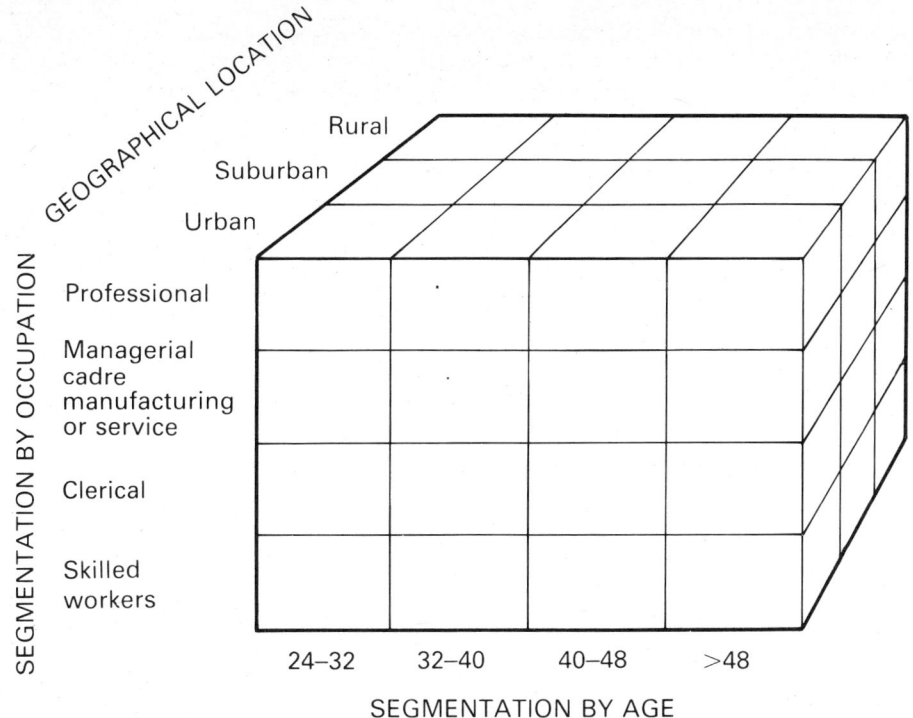

*Note:* Each cell can be broken down further; for example,
         Professional into doctors, lawyers, architects, and so on.

**Figure 4.2   Multidimensional segmentation matrix/morphology (4 × 4 × 3 = 48 cells)**

spend the kind of money which demonstrates affiliation to the group. Yet it is very much a socioeconomic niche within a well-defined socioeconomic broader segment.

Figure 4.2 illustrates in a diagrammatic form the kind of analysis which one can undertake in this regard. The idea is to build a matrix or even a three-dimensional cellular 'morphology' listing the various dimensions that interact in the market-place. Each cell represents a potential niche based on socioeconomic dimensions and needs to be measured and evaluated. It is a disciplined way of identifying as many segmentation options for analysis as possible. Similar exercises can be undertaken in relation to other segmentation bases discussed hereunder.

## Demography

This can be a fertile area for segmentation strategy search. The analysis of demographic data such as age, sex, regional differences, and so on, is capable of considerable manipulation with the view of locating gaps in the market, where needs are not currently catered for. Currently the UK population is ageing, but there are substantial regional differences. Are there thus opportunities for say house builders in developing 'sheltered' housing with a regional focus. Moreover, one can combine demographic and socioeconomic parameters in order to enrich the field of search.

## Usage rate

In every market and in every business one expects to encounter customers who buy products at different rates. In consumer goods one would expect to find 'heavy users' of beer or cigarettes as against 'light users'. In service industries one normally finds 'heavy users' of airlines as against 'light users'. The former travel frequently; the latter intermittently. In industrial goods, too, one can discover such patterns.

It is a mistake to think that the 'heavy user' is automatically the more attractive segment. Bearing in mind that good marketing must always be based on the 'horses for courses' principle, for some companies the ability to cater for the 'light user' must offer a most attractive segmentation route. Indeed, it is not always the mass supplier who represents the most successful company.

## Behavioural patterns

One of the reasons why students of marketing have to spend so much time learning about consumer behaviour is the fact that a good understanding of behavioural patterns can form a fertile basis upon which to segment markets. 'Security seekers' are clearly a better segment for insurance companies than those who feel permanently secure (do such people really exist?).

'Vain' people represent a better target segment for certain types of goods, such as fashion products, contact lenses, high-quality cosmetics, and so on. 'Intellectuals' (or those who consider themselves as such) are more likely to be interested in 'culture holidays' and may represent a fruitful segment for development.

Venturesome consumers tend to seek newly launched products rather than those that have been in existence for a long time.

In the DIY market one must recognize that not all customers are equally skilful in the use of their hands. Unfortunately most companies assume that a person who has opted for the 'Do-it-yourself' route is by definition a consumer with considerable manual dexterity. In practice the market is full of clumsy operators who would welcome 'Clumsy DIY' products.

'Hypochondriacs' represent a rich market for empathetic marketers. 'Taste' is another behavioural factor which offers segmentation opportunities. The marketer who assumes that everybody has the same taste or that what appeals to members of the marketing team is automatically a marketable commodity is running a great risk of failure. We know that exquisite design is often only attractive to the select few and at the same time, frustrating as it may sound to people of good taste, poor design appeals to the masses.

'Birds of a feather flock together' is an appropriate proverb when seeking to identify strategic segmentation openings. Knowingly or unknowingly people tend to imitate their peers. Through a careful analysis of the behavioural patterns of peer groups the creative marketer can locate valuable market segments upon which no other marketing organizations have showered their attention and affection.

In this connection it is always useful to try to identify the 'typology' or 'profile' of members of segments under analysis. If one accepts the thesis that considerable behavioural conformity exists among members of a peer group, it should not be too difficult to discover a number of characteristics that typify the behavioural patterns of people in such a group. A myriad of 'tell-tale' signals can exist. All one needs to do is to observe members of the group with great care and attention to detail.

The ability to detect the 'signals' that characterize members of a group can open highly novel segmentation opportunities for development. This concept can apply to consumer and industrial products alike. For example, owners of certain models of cars often represent a fertile segment to whom other products can be successfully sold, although they are totally unrelated to the car business.

In the industrial sector analytical observation has shown that managers who buy a lesser-known but much cheaper IBM-clone computer manifest a certain amount of venturesomeness and independence of judgement which makes them an attractive segment for other type of equipment. The nexus may be spurious but the underlying behavioural pattern similar. If a relationship between the availability of a specific computer and other buying desires can be established beyond all doubt, a most creative segmentation strategy can be formulated: a list of all the owners of the Model X computer in question can be compiled from published sources and a marketing programme aimed at such a target group developed.

## Use/purpose for purchase

Most products are bought for a variety of uses and purposes. Rare is the product which is limited to one solitary application. Thus, for example, picture frames can be used in a myriad of ways:

- decorative purposes at home
- decorative purposes in offices and commercial premises
- in institutional establishments such as hospitals, schools, airports, and so on
- restaurants and hotels
- complying with legal requirements to show certificates and/or official documents in public places
- during exhibitions and/or fairs
- gifts or presents
- sales aids and other promotional material.

Many other 'use' segments can be discovered and/or conceived.

Similarly in the pharmaceuticals industry drugs can be segmented by:

- the disease that the drug seeks to alleviate
- age groupings
- allergies
- animals as against humans.

In the industrial market one can take an example from the aluminium business. Aluminium extrusions serve a large number of applications and purposes. To name only a few:

- the manufacture of window frames
- cladding
- suspended ceilings
- partitions
- furniture
- packaging.

Each one of these applications represents a market segment. Dozens of others exist and should be identified and analysed. In practice what is an attractive segment for Company A is not necessarily equally attractive for Company B, and this is what makes the whole concept so valuable.

## *Benefit segmentation*

Earlier in this book it was emphasized that the customer seeks benefits rather than products. What this statement implies is that products are only the vehicles for the delivery of benefits. Products come and go, the product life-cycle will see to that. However, the underlying needs of the market are unlikely to change that much. Hence the need in marketing to focus on benefits.

One crucial finding that comes out of any analysis of the benefit structure of markets is that different customers seek different benefits. Thus there exists the opportunity to segment markets according to the benefits that particular type of customers seek. For example, one well-known study found that for an everyday product such as toothpaste there can be half-a-dozen different benefit segments. These segments included the 'dental health seeker', that is those who used toothpaste primarily to reduce decay; another group was the cosmetic segment, who primarily sought the benefit of white, attractive teeth. Still further segments were the 'value for money' segment and the 'fresh breath' segment.

In other words, it becomes possible to see a way in which specific products can be designed and promoted to specific benefit segments. This concept of benefit segmentation extends to all types of markets. For example, in industrial marketing we frequently find that different users seek widely different benefits. Take computers for example; here it is possible to take the same physical product but emphasize different features to different benefit segments. This type of segmentation enables the corporate manufacturer to assemble different marketing 'packages' with appeals that will have attraction to specific types of customers.

Obviously to develop successful benefit segmentation strategies requires a careful analysis of the market and the customers. Benefits are perceptual and thus research into customer motivations is an essential first step towards identifying the real benefit segments in the market-place.

## Attitudes

The attitudes of one individual differ from those of the next person. Attitudes are the result of years of socialization through pressures from one's peer groups, education at school and at university, one's own self-development activities and the impact of the media that one reads or watches.

Nevertheless, the plethora of attitudes that people manifest usually fall into fairly discrete patterns. Attitudes exist in clusters. Thus a conservative person (in the non-political sense) tends to be a loyal customer, an avid saver, an enthusiast for insurance cover against every conceivable contingency and also tends to shun new products until they have gained acceptability and some track record.

On the other hand, the person who manifests more venturesome attitudes is also more likely to experiment with new products, change patronage and take risky decisions. Altogether such a person is much more likely to respond to creative offerings than the conservative individual.

Understanding the attitudinal make-up of consumers can form a valuable basis upon which to segment markets. If the company is highly innovative in its product strategy, it can define the so-called 'innovators' as its main target market. If, on the other hand, it lags behind in product development, it might be better off to target upon the more conservative and cautious type of customer. Both strategies are valid depending on which company one works for and the specific inventory of strengths and weaknesses that one has identified for each company. The innovative company would be unwise to target its effort upon the 'stick-in-the-mud' customer and the 'laggard' company would be silly to seek to gain the loyalty of the venturesome and experimental consumer. 'Horses for courses' is once again the appropriate maxim.

These were just a few examples of bases upon which markets can be segmented. The list can be expanded tenfold. The main message for top management is that the number of strategic segmentation options that can be found is almost limitless. During the strategy search process considerable impetus must be placed from the top towards the identification of as many bases for segmentation options as possible. It is useful to remember that quite often the basis for segmentation that looks bizarre at first sight is the winner in the commercial battlefield!

# Strategic options

It was suggested earlier that one of the fundamental decisions that a firm's strategists must reach is whether the firm should apply its marketing attention and resources to one or a few niches or operate as an 'all things to all men' enterprise. The former company recognizes the existence of segmentation opportunities and seeks to exploit them to the best advantage. The latter prefers to cater for the total market regardless of the segments and sub-segments that may exist in it.

A third option is where the company decides to undertake a hybrid approach: it clusters customers into discrete groupings and seeks to meet the needs of all these clusters, thus covering a wider market. However, each such cluster is catered for with a different approach and 'marketing mix'. This option is the most expensive inasmuch as the company finds itself involved with a large range of offerings, heavy marketing costs and probably the management of a complex range of channels of distribution.

The choice of the strategic route implied by the three approaches can only be reached after the firm has undertaken a comprehensive analysis of its own capabilities, competences and strengths on the one hand and its shortcomings and weaknesses on the other. Such an audit must be practical and totally honest. It is not an exercise in self-congratulation but a realistic appraisal of the firm's true talents. An insurance company that has always operated through brokers and has never attempted to establish direct communication with the customers should accept the fact that such a weakness exists. It must not assume that by simply ignoring the existence of this shortcoming it will disappear. Weaknesses do not disappear by themselves. They can only be corrected or removed as a result of a concerted effort and the planned injection of resources. The simple rule is that segmentation and positioning strategies must be masterminded around an honest and realistic perception of the most attractive options which are at the same time the most compatible ones with the firm's carefully evaluated capabilities.

The strategic options described above can be illustrated in diagrammatic form. Figure 4.3 suggests that a market can be segmented into five distinct parts. As the bar chart shows, the segments are not of equal size. Some segments are large and some are relatively small. For the purpose of the illustration the segments are referred to as A, B, C, D and E.

Let us assume that the company has analysed and quantified the size and value of each one of the five segments. Moreover let us also

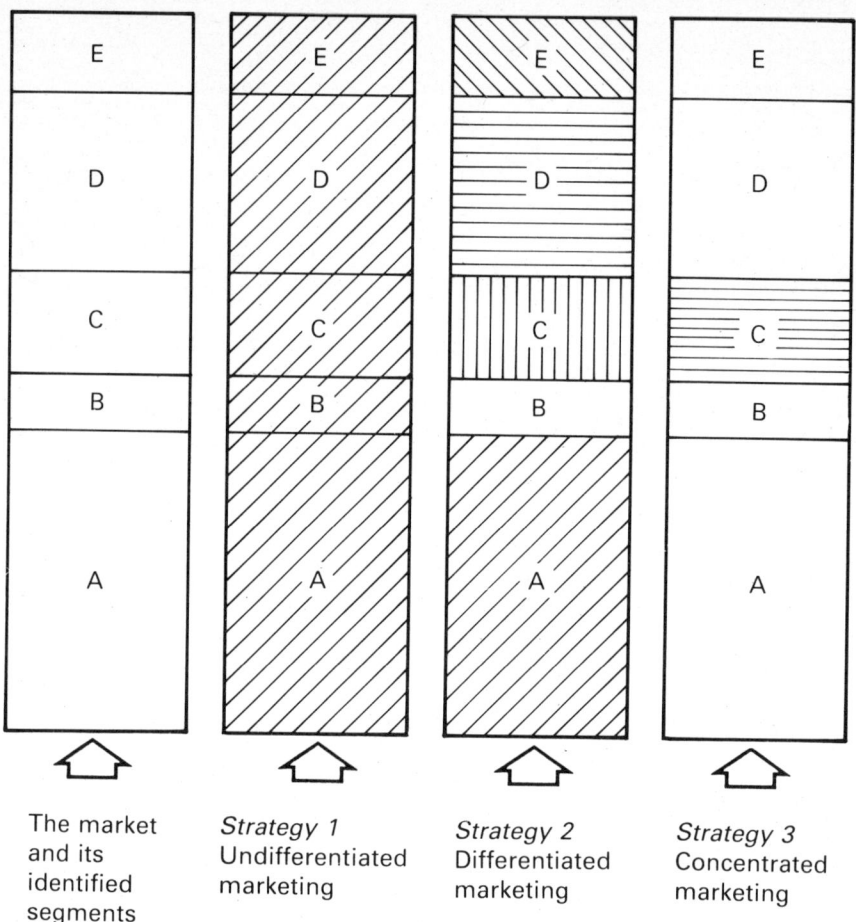

| The market and its identified segments | *Strategy 1* Undifferentiated marketing | *Strategy 2* Differentiated marketing | *Strategy 3* Concentrated marketing |

**Figure 4.3  Market segments and the strategic options**

assume that the firm has evaluated its ability to compete effectively in all or a number of segments shown. At this stage three optional strategies are open to the company:

## *Strategy 1: undifferentiated marketing*

This means treating the whole market and all the segments in it in the same way. The product, price, promotion, selling activities and distribution will be the same for every customer in the market-place regardless of the segment he or she belongs to.

This can be a perfectly acceptable strategy in a given set of circumstances. It is particularly appropriate if the following conditions apply:

- where the products are highly innovative and probably at the early stage of the life-cycle
- when the company enjoys the protection of a strong patent
- when evidence exists that consumption habits and taste are homogeneous among all the segments identified
- where the company is strong enough to attain a quick and aggressive penetration of the market thus attaining the full benefits of the 'experience curve' and cost advantage
- where the product or technology are likely to be so short-lived that one must try to achieve an investment recovery in as short a time as possible.

### Strategy 2: differentiated marketing

Here the company recognizes the existence of a variety of segments and seeks to cater for all or most of them. The 'marketing mix' is adjusted whenever appropriate. If necessary the product is modified to meet the specific needs of members of each segment. The communication mix (namely the promotion and selling activities) and the price are altered in response to identified needs and expectations of the identified sub-markets. Moreover, it is rare for the same channels of distribution to be equally effective in relation to all the segments that the company seeks to penetrate.

Considerable marketing resources are normally required when a company decides to undertake a broadly based differentiation programme. Undoubtedly it is a much more expensive task to plan for a multi-segment marketing strategy than for a single-segment campaign or an undifferentiated approach to the whole market.

The decision to differentiate a marketing programme is a vital one in the career of a company and should not be taken lightly. Strictly speaking, where there is no justification for differentiation it is probably wiser not to choose such a route. If an airline is very successful with a one-class offering and is likely to remain so, there is little reason for adding a 'First Class', a 'Business Class' or a 'Cabin Class'.

Nevertheless, differentiation may be the appropriate route in the following situations:

- where the company is large and enjoys a dominant position in the market-place

- where the products have reached maturity and through differentiation it is hoped to increase their attractiveness among the various segments identified
- where the market is extremely competitive and differentiation coupled with innovation can improve the acceptability of the product among market sub-groups (e.g. a watch designed for joggers may have a greater appeal to them than an ordinary time-keeping watch; as long as such a product enjoys uniqueness the manufacturer of such a watch is likely to gain a major penetration of this specific segment)
- where the company needs to increase its overall market share as part of a defensive or an offensive strategy.

In certain circumstances failure to differentiate may leave the company vulnerable to the onslaught of creative marketers who may decide to position themselves in one or more attractive segments. For example, a large television manufacturer may be risking the company's future if it ignores the existence of a leisure/out-of-doors segment inasmuch as a successful penetration of such a market by competition can entail a dual danger:

- It provides the smaller competitor, who opts for this segment, with a vantage position from which to attack the larger market.
- The portion of the average consumer's disposable income which is spent on television sets will be split between ordinary and portable sets thus diminishing the funds available for the ordinary set market. Abdicating from the latter can entail a hazardous diminution in one's current market.

## Strategy 3: concentrated marketing

As the expression implies, the firm's strategists here recognize the company's limitations within the competitive arena in which it operates. Rather than fight in the total market, they decide to concentrate upon one carefully selected market niche. The risk associated with such a strategy can be high, especially where the company has failed to do its homework adequately.

The whole concept is based on the desire to operate in an area which is not infested with competitors and which at the same time represents a healthy market opportunity. However, if the company's strategic thinkers fail to validate their hypotheses, they run the grave risk of 'placing all their eggs in one basket'. On the other hand, if all the facts and figures justify the proposed plan to target on a limited albeit profitable segment, the outcome may be a worthwhile one.

Again there are occasions when the concentrated marketing route is the most desirable within the context of a strategy search exercise:

- when the company's resources are limited and it has to compete against one or more powerful competitors
- when the company enters into a heavily congested market for the first time
- when the market niche appears to be highly synergistic with the existing business of the organization
- altogether, where the firm is enjoying a highly visible image in a given market segment it makes good sense to try to capitalize upon such a strength.

It often happens that a firm adopts a concentrated marketing strategy without realizing that it has chosen such a route. It simply happens as a result of a historical commitment to a specific segment or some specialized knowledge that might exist among the company's management. A manufacturer of plastic sheeting who has decided to concentrate all its marketing effort on the car industry can be rightly said to have adopted a concentrated marketing strategy. Such an organization must from time to time take stock of its standing in such a segment. It must refrain from institutionalizing a past decision without reflecting upon its longer-term implications. The decision might have been wrong in the first place and the company might have developed an easier and more profitable segment. It is worth remembering that this is precisely what the planning process aims to achieve: identifying mistakes and helping to develop a better and easier future and not just condoning past strategic commitments.

In this connection it is always useful to try to understand, wherever possible, the logic that was applied in the first place to the choice of the original positioning route. Running a business is first and foremost a logical process. The selection of strategies for the future direction of an organization must also be based on common sense. It is therefore important to try to understand the logic of the past before applying it to the future. Obviously, if the quality of the thinking in the distant past was unsound, there is little reason for perpetuating the outcome of such a process into the future. A strategy of concentration on a market niche is probably one of the most important decisions in a firm's existence. It must be examined with great analytical care during the planning process. The risk of concentration on a segment which is commercially unattractive or of short marketing duration is too great to be allowed to continue by default.

It is also worth remembering that a creative concentration strategy on a niche can be a valuable stepping-stone towards an onslaught on the whole market. The successful management of a small albeit profitable segment can give the organization the resources and the competitive cutting edge which will enable it to broaden its marketing vistas. As the company grows (in relative terms to its competitors) it can cast its attention to a differentiation and re-positioning strategy. Once it reaches a certain level of success and size, it often has to increase its catchment markets beyond the original 'little pond' it chose for itself in the earlier years.

In practice this happens very frequently but unfortunately it seldom happens as a result of clearly formulated long-range plans. Small and relatively underresourced firms stand a better chance of success with a concentrated marketing strategy. Medium-sized organizations can widen their perspectives with a partial differentiation programme, whilst the 'big boys' can maximize their opportunities through a highly differentiated marketing strategy. Knowing who one is and what one is capable of doing is the secret.

# Selecting a strategy: limitations to choice

It will be evident that a large number of segments and niches upon which viable marketing strategies can be based ought to be assembled and examined during the planning stage. In fact the bigger the choice, the better the chance that a number of very innovative options may be finally chosen. It is better to have too many options than too few. The total creative talent of an organization must be harnessed during this phase of the strategic explorations.

However, one of the dangers that may confront a company during the search for segmentation strategies is that excessive stimulation and enthusiasm on the part of the participants in this exercise may override their commercial wisdom and analytical judgement. It is useful to bear in mind that not every segment idea represents a viable proposition. A segment may look attractive from a novelty viewpoint yet be commercially disastrous. Later on we shall consider a number of evaluation procedures that the firm's planners should try to follow before committing the company's resources to a strategic route.

Meanwhile a number of valuable safeguards to niche choice must be briefly discussed. Their absence should be treated as a warning signal to those involved in strategic explorations relating to segmentation and positioning activities.

## Measurement and quantification

Before choosing a segment one must carry out detailed investigations pertaining to its size, attractiveness and ease of penetration. Many creative and imaginative segmentation strategies have failed in the past because in the course of the planning phase the marketers have failed to measure and quantify the true size of the opportunity under consideration. One normally takes it for granted that total markets must be measured and quantified. Clearly it is equally, if not more, important to attempt to measure the size of sub-markets when one is seeking to operate in a narrower part of the market. This is particularly true if one is heading for a 'concentrated marketing' approach. The risk of not knowing the exact size of a niche is far greater than when a company is marketing its products and/or services to all and sundry.

The more obvious and traditional segments are usually easy to measure. Unfortunately the more original the segment, the harder it is to quantify. If the information infrastructure of the country has not heard of such a segment, the likelihood of finding published data on it is small. This often represents a Catch-22 dilemma: if data aiding measurability is easily available, the likelihood is that most well-informed strategists are aware of the segmentation opportunities implied; if measurability is difficult or impossible, quantifying the niche opportunities is problematic and therefore selecting such vague strategic options must be avoided.

This constraint is particularly true where the nature of the segment is somewhat vague as, for instance, when the niche hypothesis is based on behavioural factors. It is rare to find well-researched and well-presented data about behavioural patterns in a market. It is quite difficult to find published information about how many 'hypochondriacs' exist in a given country. Similarly it is virtually impossible to measure the number of 'self-centred' men of 27–32 age group either from published data or through research.

A valuable method for overcoming measurability constraints in such awkward situations is to endeavour to establish a 'nexus' between the dimension that one wants to measure and a linked factor which happens to be more easily quantifiable. Thus, if one wants to measure the size of the '27–32 self-centred male' segment one must try to identify the typical consumption patterns of such individuals. If one can establish through sampling methods that the typical possessions of such people are, for instance, specific car models, car telephones, certain types of watches or pens, and so on, one can measure the latter and derive some 'tell-tale' quantification of the segment size. This is no different from the process of measuring the attendance in a conference centre without having access to the grounds. All one has to do is count the number of cars in the car park. Clearly the results are crude and may be distorted by the fact that some people have come by public transport or on foot. Nevertheless, if one assumes that *Homo sapiens* behaves in a fairly regular pattern, and if one conducts such a simple car counting process at regular intervals, an increase or decrease in the number of cars does provide a quantifiable pattern of measurement.

This kind of correlation analysis opens an exciting opportunity to measure the unmeasurable and in the hands of the creative analyst can yield useful output. Yet it is important to recognize and remember at all times that in the final analysis a segment which is incapable of measurement is less attractive than one which is fully explored and quantified.

## Commercial and financial viability

Managers who have been bitten by the bug of segmentation often lose sight of the dangers of oversegmenting one's marketing vistas. If a microcomputer manufacturer decides to avoid the mass market and concentrate all his effort on a special 'package' for pathologists, he must calculate the financial viability of such a strategy. The firm may well discover that having achieved a 100 per cent market share in this niche it is facing a financial disaster.

Segmentation can be an exciting strategy but the commercial realities of running a business must be kept in mind at all times. Achieving a mass-market share of a segment is only attractive when the financial and commercial objectives of the firm are also met.

In other words, before recommending a positioning strategy to one's colleagues one must evaluate the financial implications of each option. At this stage one does not need to embark on copious in-depth analysis. What is needed is a quick business screening procedure to evaluate the viability of each segmentation option. Such procedures will be discussed in the final part of this chapter.

## *Accessibility*

The word 'accessibility' covers a multitude of issues. A segment may or may not be accessible to a marketing company for a myriad of reasons:

- The channels of distribution are either not in existence or are unwilling to handle the company's products.
- The promotional infrastructure in the market-place is not geared to performing an effective communication task with members of the segment under scrutiny.

If, for instance, one decides to market left-handed scissors for left-handed people, the following points arise:

- What kind of shops will agree to sell such a product?
- Where can one advertise the availability of such a novelty without incurring astronomical promotional costs? Of course, if a magazine devoted to the needs and problems of left-handed people does exist the problem is immediately solved. Accessibility is assured.
- There are situations where accessibility cannot be attained as a result of emotional, ethical or legal barriers to communication. It is better to recognize these barriers at an early stage and before one starts spending time and resources on developing business plans which ultimately may have to be aborted.

## **Overview**

Traditionally market segmentation has been left to the marketing department, but it is the contention in this chapter that such an important component of a company's success must be the business of senior management.

Central to conducting a market segmentation analysis is recognizing the company's strengths, weaknesses, opportunities and threats to discover how the company can thrive in a competitive environment. By conducting such an analysis the company can find a 'gap' or 'niche' in the market in which to excel.

A creative technique called 'mapping' is described which can identify congested areas of market activity and reveal gaps which present a positioning opportunity. The company must then identify the base or bases upon which the market can be segmented. With creativity and imagination, the list is almost endless, but several are explored here: socioeconomic segments, demography, usage rate, behavioural patterns, use/purpose for purchase, benefit segmentation, attitudes.

Whatever base is used, a company must decide on its main strategic option. Will it concentrate on a few niches or decide on a mass approach, or will it attempt a combination of the two?

Any chosen segment must satisfy three criteria: it must be capable of measurement and quantification; it must represent a sufficiently large opportunity to be commercially and financially viable; and it must be accessible.

# 5 The strategic planning process

## The need for strategic marketing planning

Marketing's contribution to business success in manufacturing, distribution or merchanting activities lies in its commitment to detailed analysis of future opportunities to meet customer needs and a wholly professional approach to selling to well-defined market segments those products or services that deliver the sought-after benefits. Whilst prices and discounts are important, as are advertising and promotion, the link with engineering through the product is paramount.

Such a commitment and activities must not be mistaken for budgets and forecasts. Those, of course, we need and we have already got. Our accounting colleagues have long since seen to that. Put quite bluntly, the process of marketing planning is concerned with identifying, in the longer term, what will be selling and to whom, to give revenue budgets and sales forecasts any chance of achievement. Furthermore, changes of achievement are a function of how good our intelligence services are; and how well suited are our strategies; and how well we are led.

One is continuously haunted by the large number of disorientated directors and senior managers in many sectors of industry. The simple environment of the 1960s and early 1970s, characterized by growth and the easy marketability of products and services, has now been replaced by an increasingly complex and abrasive environment, coupled with static or declining markets.

The difficulty faced by many directors stems from the realization that the old methods no longer work. Even worse, it is beginning to dawn on many that in those halcyon years they were hardly managing at all – rather they were being dragged along by the momentum of growth, and all they were doing was riding the wave. Of course, it was always necessary, even in those days, to understand the day-to-day operational basics and manage them well, but there wasn't the same need for a disciplined, systematic approach to the market.

Figure 5.1 shows a matrix in which the horizontal axis represents strategy as a continuum from ineffective to effective. The vertical axis represents tactics on a continuum from inefficient to efficient. Those firms with an effective strategy and efficient tactics continue to thrive, whilst those with an effective strategy but inefficient tactics have merely survived. Many such firms have devoted much of their time and energy to shedding unnecessary and inefficient peripheral activities and are once more moving towards the top right-hand box. Many, of course, have gone bankrupt.

Those firms to the left of the matrix are doomed. It is in circumstances like this where the old-style management fails. Sadly, many of these old-style experiential managers have resorted to their 'Action Man' kits, which is accompanied by much cost-cutting and bullying, often referred to more classically as 'Anorexia Industrialo-sa' (the excessive desire to be leaner and fitter, leading to emaciation and eventual death).

By failing to grasp the nettle of strategic orientation, many directors have become, and many more will become, casualties and

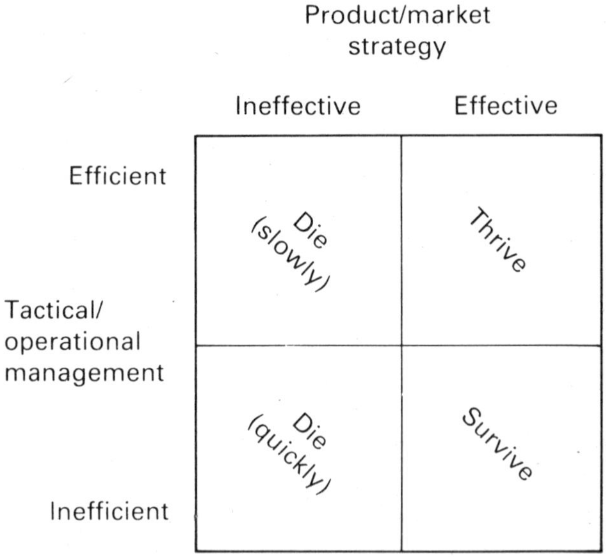

**Figure 5.1   Efficiency versus effectiveness**

their place will be taken by a new breed who are comfortable driving with the new orientation. Already companies led by chief executives with a proactive orientation that stretches beyond the end of the current fiscal year have begun to show results visibly better than the old reactive companies with only a short-term vision.

Increasingly we meet chief executives and directors who have grasped, or who are trying to grasp, the absolute necessity of having a vision of where their companies should be going, with this direction properly articulated in business plans that identify and develop their distinctive competence. Where this isn't happening, plans are developed from a purely financial basis, are mainly extrapolative and can be likened to a sailor steering by the wake in busy and choppy waters. Not only that, but since most operational managers prefer selling the products they find easiest to sell to the customers that offer the least line of resistance, this approach is tantamount to an extrapolation of the firm's own inefficiencies. Certainly, however, this approach has very little to do with the business of properly understood market-centred opportunities. On the other hand, it is easy to understand why so many companies prefer this mode of management.

Many strategic planning departments of the 1970s, bulging with highly paid management scientists, wafted out the results of their models and brainstorming in a platonic haze that was inevitably distanced from the 'coal-face' and the real world of operational managers. The gap between long-term strategic and short-term operational plans grew wider, until finally the bubble burst with the onset of the recession, and much of this kind of planning was exposed as the farce that it has always been. Alas, the recession was also accompanied by a return to old well-tried-and-tested management methods as the 'Action Man' kits were brought out yet again. Strategic planning was out and the hobnail boot brigade returned, at least for a time.

Now, however, the new breed of top executives are taking everyone in their company through an often traumatic period of cultural change from operational to strategic modes. These people have rightly dismissed the arrant nonsenses which arose out of earlier approaches to strategic planning and which understandably got planning a bad name.

The new emerging culture places a much greater emphasis on scanning the external environment, the early identification of forces emanating from it, and developing appropriate strategic responses. The difference this time round is that all levels of management are involved, with the resulting intelligence coming from the market

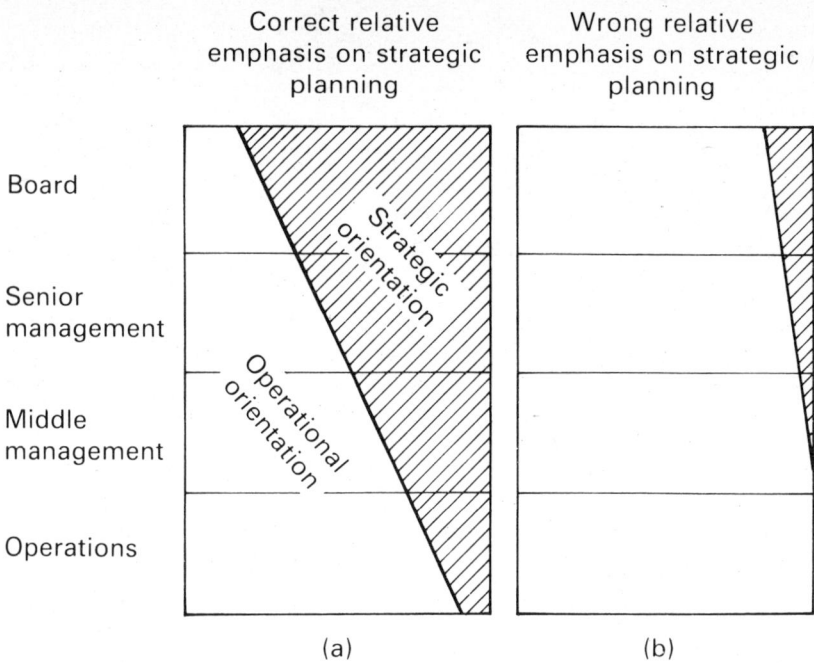

**Figure 5.2    The strategy–operations balance**

rather than from the heads of a remote group of planners with little or no operational involvement.

Figure 5.2(b) shows the old style of company in which very little attention is paid by any level of management to strategy. It will be seen that lower levels of management do not get involved at all, whilst the directors spend most of their time on operational issues. Figure 5.2(a) shows that all levels of management are involved to some extent in strategy formulation.

It is not difficult to pinpoint the companies that have not adopted (or will not adopt) the new strategic orientation. They reorganize with monotonous regularity because they don't know what else to do. This preoccupation with organizational structure is likely to be fatal in many cases, simply because there isn't the same slack in the system as there was in the 1960s and 1970s. In those days the directors could amuse themselves endlessly putting the fear of God into their subordinates with their interminable tinkering with structure. Not so today.

Only when a company has developed a strategy towards its market-place should its organization structure even be considered –

and then it should be designed to reflect its strategic thrust in the external market. So, strategy before structure should be the basic orientation rather than the more usual structure before strategy.

There are three distinct yet interdependent stages involved in developing a strategic marketing capability in an organization:

1  Establish a disciplined framework (or logic) for undertaking the marketing planning process.
2  Underpin this framework with a meaningful marketing intelligence function.
3  Undertake the necessary steps inside the organization to convert the words on paper (plans) into actionable propositions on the ground. When this behaviour is being achieved on a consistent basis, then a new culture has been established.

These three stages are not achieved without considerable pain to participating executives because they are being called on to think and act in ways which are radically different from the experiential norms of earlier years.

If they make the transition successfully, they will feel ownership over their strategic and operational plans and will thus ensure that they are implemented with enthusiasm and dedication. But what about those companies that use outside consultants to formulate their strategic position? This approach is becoming increasingly invalid because little or no *residual* is left behind in the organization after the task is completed. Little or no *learning* can take place unless chief executives themselves are actively driving the process of strategy formulation, sharing the pain with their associates and achieving ownership of the results through this active participative role.

## Role of the chief executive in strategic marketing planning

When the role of the chief executive in strategic marketing planning was examined in our research, it was found that few have a clear perception of the

- purposes and methods of planning
- proper assignments of planning responsibilities throughout the organization
- proper structures and staffing of the planning department
- talent and skills required in an effective planning department.

The role of the chief executive is generally agreed as being to

- define the organizational framework
- ensure that strategic analysis covers critical factors
- maintain the balance between short- and long-term results
- display his commitment to planning
- provide the entrepreneurial dynamic to overcome bureaucracy
- build this dynamic into the planning operation (motivation).

In respect of planning, his principal role is to open up the planning loop by means of his personal intervention. The main purpose of this is to act as a catalyst for the entrepreneurial dynamic within his organization, which can so easily decay through bureaucratization.

## What is strategic marketing planning?

Let us begin by reminding ourselves what strategic marketing planning is. It is a logical sequence and a series of activities leading to the setting of marketing objectives and the formulation of plans for achieving them. It is a management process.

Conceptually the process is very simple. Strategic marketing planning by means of a planning system is, *per se*, little more than a structured way of identifying a range of options for the company, of making them explicit in writing, of formulating marketing objectives which are consistent with the company's overall objectives and of scheduling and costing out the specific activities most likely to bring about the achievement of the objectives. *It is the systemization of this process which is distinctive and which lies at the heart of the theory of strategic marketing planning.*

What are the benefits of strategic marketing planning? The main ones are:

- co-ordination of the activities of many individuals whose actions are interrelated over time
- identification of expected developments
- preparedness to meet changes when they occur
- minimization of non-rational responses to the unexpected
- better communication among executives
- minimization of conflicts among individuals which would result in a subordination of the goals of the company to those of the individual.

Whilst these benefits will not necessarily always follow as a result of the adoption of strategic marketing planning, it is likely that the *disadvantages* and problems of traditional budgeting and forecasting systems will be avoided.

The following are the operating problems most commonly arising from a reliance on traditional sales forecasting and budgeting procedures in the absence of a marketing planning system:

- lost opportunities for profit
- meaningless numbers in long-range plans
- unrealistic objectives
- lack of actionable market information
- interfunctional strife
- management frustration
- proliferation of products and markets
- wasted promotional expenditure
- pricing confusion
- growing vulnerability to environmental change
- loss of control over the business.

It is not difficult to see the connection between all of these problems. However, what is perhaps not apparent from the list is that each of these operational problems is in fact a symptom of a much larger problem which emanates from the way in which the objectives of a firm are set.

The objective-setting process of a business is central to marketing effectiveness. What the research has demonstrated conclusively is that it is inadequacies in the objective-setting process which lie at the heart of many of the problems of British companies. We frequently encounter reference to profit as being the only objective necessary to successful business performance. There is in the minds of many businessmen the assumption that in order to be commercially successful all that is necessary is for the 'boss' to set profit targets, to decentralize the firm into groups of similar activities, and then to make managers accountable for achieving those profits. However, even though most British companies have made the making of 'profit' almost the sole objective, many of our industries have gone into decline, and ironically, there has also been a decline in real profitability. There are countless examples of companies pursuing decentralized profit goals that have failed miserably.

Here it is necessary to focus attention on what so many companies appear to be bad at – that is, determining strategies for matching what the firm is good at with properly researched market-centred opportunities and then scheduling and costing out what has to be done to achieve these objectives. There is little evidence of a deep understanding of what it is that companies can do better than their competitors or of how their distinctive competence can be matched with the needs of certain customer groups. Instead, overall volume increases and minimum rates of return on investment are frequently applied to all products and markets, irrespective of market share, market growth rate or the longevity of the product life-cycle. Indeed, there is a lot of evidence to show that many companies are in trouble today precisely because their decentralized units manage their business only for the current profit-and-loss account, often at the expense of giving up valuable and hard-earned market share, failing to invest in R&D and running down the current business.

Thus financial objectives, whilst being essential measures of the desired performance of a company, are of little practical help since they say nothing about *how* the results are to be achieved. The same applies to sales forecasts and budgets, which are *not* marketing objectives and strategies. Understanding the real meaning and significance of marketing objectives helps managers to know what information they need to enable them to think through the implications of choosing one or more positions in the market. Finding the right words to describe the logic of marketing objectives and strategies is infinitely more difficult than writing down numbers on a piece of paper and leaving the strategies implicit. This lies at the heart of the problem. For clearly, a numbers-orientated system will not encourage managers to think in a structured way about strategically relevant market segments, nor will it encourage the collection, analysis and synthesis of actionable market data. In the absence of such activities within operating units, it is unlikely that headquarters will have much other than intuition and 'feel' to use as a basis for decisions about the management of scarce resources.

## How can these problems be overcome?

A major difficulty is of how to get managers throughout an organization thinking beyond the horizon of the current year's operations. This applies universally to all types and sizes of company. Even chief executives of small companies find difficulty in breaking out of the fetters of the current profit-and-loss account.

The problem, particularly in large companies, is that managers who are evaluated and rewarded on the basis of current operations find difficulty in concerning themselves about the corporate future. This is exacerbated by behavioural issues, in the sense that it is safer, and more rewarding personally, for a manager to do what he knows best, which in most cases is to manage his *current* range of products and customers in order to make the *current* year's budget.

Unfortunately, long-range sales forecasting systems do not provide the answer. This kind of extrapolative approach fails to solve the problems of identifying precisely what has to be done today to ensure success in the future. Exactly the same problem exists in both large diversified companies and in small undiversified companies, except that in the former the problem is magnified and multiplied by the complexities of distance, hierarchical levels of management and diversity of operations. Nevertheless, the problem is fundamentally the same.

Events that affect economic performance in a business come from so many directions, and in so many forms, that it is impossible for any manager to be precise about how they interact in the form of problems to be overcome and opportunities to be exploited. The best a manager can do is to form a reasoned view about how they have affected the past, how they will develop in the future and what action needs to be taken over a period of time to enable the company to prepare itself for the expected changes. The problem is *how* to get managers to formulate their thoughts about these things, for until they have, it is unlikely that any objectives that are set will have much relevance or meaning.

Accordingly, they need some system which will help them to think in a structured way about problem formulation. It is the provision of such a rational framework to help them to make explicit their intuitive economic models of the business that is almost totally lacking from the forecasting and budgeting systems of most companies. It is apparent that in the absence of any such synthesized and simplified views of the business, setting meaningful objectives for the future seems like an insurmountable problem, and this in turn encourages the perpetuation of systems involving merely the extrapolation of numbers. There is also substantial evidence that those companies that provide procedures for this process, however informal, have gone some considerable way to overcoming this problem. Although the possible number of analyses of business situations is infinite, procedural approaches help managers through-out an organization at least to consider the essential elements of problem definition in a structured way. This applies even to difficult foreign markets, where data and information is hard to come by, and even to markets which are being managed by agents, who find that these structured approaches, properly managed, help *their* businesses as well as those of their principals.

However, there are two further major advantages enjoyed by these companies. First, the level of management frustration is lower and motivation is higher because the system provides a method of reaching agreement on such difficult matters as an assessment of the company's distinctive competence and the nature of the competitive environment. The internecine disputes and frustration which we all experience so often in our business lives is largely the result of an almost total absence of the means of discussing these issues and of reaching agreement on them. If a manager's boss does not understand what his environmental problems are, what his strengths and weaknesses are, nor what he is trying to achieve, and in the absence of any structured procedures and common terminology that can be used and understood by everybody, communications will be poor and the incidence of frustration will be higher.

Second, some form of standardized approach which is understood by all considerably improves the ability of headquarters management not only to understand the problems of individual operating units but also to react to them in a constructive and helpful way. This is because they receive information in a way which enables them to form a meaningful overview of total company activities, and this provides a rational basis for resource allocation.

To summarize, a structured approach to situation analysis is necessary, irrespective of the size or complexity of the organization. Such a system should:

- ensure that comprehensive consideration is given to the definition of strengths and weaknesses and to problems and opportunities
- ensure that a logical framework is used for the presentation of the key issues arising from this analysis.

Very few companies have planning systems which possess these characteristics. Those that do, manage to cope with their environment more effectively than those that do not. They find it easier to set meaningful marketing objectives, are more confident about the future, enjoy greater control over the business and react less on a piecemeal basis to ongoing events. In short, they suffer fewer operational problems and are as a result more effective organizations.

## The marketing planning process

So far in this chapter we have made it clear that marketing planning is essential when we consider the increasingly hostile and complex environment in which companies operate. Hundreds of external and internal factors interact in a bafflingly complex way to effect our ability to achieve profitable sales. Managers of a company have to have some understanding or view about how all these variables interact, and managers try to be rational about their business decisions, no matter how important intuition and experience are as contributory factors in this process of rationality.

Most managers accept that some kind of formalized procedure for marketing planning helps sharpen this rationality so as to reduce the complexity of business operations and add a dimension of realism to the company's hopes for the future. Because it is so difficult, however, most companies rely only on sales forecasting and budgeting systems. All too frequently, however, they bear little relationship to the real opportunities and problems facing a company. It is far more difficult to write down marketing objectives and strategies.

*The steps*

Figure 5.3 illustrates the several stages that have to be gone through in order to arrive at a marketing plan. This illustrates the difference between the *process* of marketing planning and the actual plan itself, which is the output of the process.

Experience has shown that a marketing plan should contain:

- a summary of all the principal external factors which affected the company's marketing performance during the previous year, together with a statement of the company's strengths and weaknesses *vis-à-vis* the competition – this is what we call a SWOT (i.e. strengths, weaknesses, opportunities, threats) analysis
- some assumptions about the key determinants of marketing success and failure
- overall marketing objectives and strategies
- programmes containing details of timing, responsibilities and costs, with sales forecasts and budgets.

Each of the stages illustrated in Figure 5.3 will be discussed in more detail later in this chapter. The dotted lines joining up steps 5, 6 and 7 are meant to indicate the reality of the planning process in that it is likely that each of these steps will have to be gone through more than once before final programmes can be written.

Although research has shown these marketing planning steps to

**Figure 5.3   The strategic marketing planning process**

be universally applicable, the degree to which each of the separate steps in the diagram needs to be formalized depends to a large extent on the size and nature of the company. For example, an *undiversified* company generally uses less-formalized procedures, since top management tends to have greater functional knowledge and expertise than subordinates, and because the lack of diversity of operations enables direct control to be exercised over most of the key determinates of success. Thus situation reviews, the setting of marketing objectives, and so on, are not always made explicit in writing, although these steps have to be gone through.

In contrast, in a *diversified* company it is usually not possible for top management to have greater functional knowledge and expertise than subordinate management, hence the whole planning process tends to be more formalized in order to provide a consistent discipline for those who have to make the decisions throughout the organization. Either way, however, there is now a substantial body of evidence to show that formalized planning procedures generally result in greater profitability and stability in the long term and also help to reduce friction and operational difficulties within organizations.

Where marketing planning has failed, it has generally been because companies have placed too much emphasis on the procedures themselves and the resulting paperwork, rather than on generating information useful to and consumable by management. Also, where companies relegate marketing planning to someone called a 'planner', it invariably fails, for the single reason that planning for line management cannot be delegated to a third party. The real role of the 'planner' should be to help those responsible for implementation to plan. Failure to recognize this simple fact can be disastrous. Finally, planning failures often result from companies trying too much, too quickly and without training staff in the use of procedures.

We can now look at the marketing planning process in more detail, starting with a look at the marketing audit. So far we have identified the need for marketing planning and outlined a series of steps that have to be gone through in order to arrive at a marketing plan. However, any plan will only be as good as the information on which it is based, and the marketing audit is the means by which information for planning is organized.

## What is a marketing audit?

A marketing audit is a systematic appraisal of all the external and internal factors that have affected a company's commercial performance over a defined period. Given the growing turbulence of the business environment and the shorter product life-cycles that have resulted, no-one would deny the need to stop at least once a year at a particular point in the planning cycle to try to form a reasoned view on how all the many external and internal factors have influenced performance.

Sometimes, of course, a company will conduct a marketing audit because it is in financial trouble. At times like these, management often attempts to treat the wrong symptoms, most frequently by reorganizing the company. But such measures are unlikely to be effective if there are more fundamental problems which have not been identified. Of course, if the company survived for long enough, it might eventually solve its problems through a process of elimination. Essentially, though, the argument is that problems have first to be properly defined. The audit is a means of helping to define them.

## Two kinds of variable

Any company carrying out an audit will be faced with two kinds of variable. There is the kind over which the company has no direct control, for example economic and market factors. Second, there are those over which the company has complete control, the operational variables, which are usually the firm's internal resources. This division suggests that the best way to structure an audit is in two parts, internal and external. Table 5.1 shows areas

**Table 5.1**
**Issues for inclusion in a SWOT analysis**

| External audit | | Internal audit |
|---|---|---|
| *Business and economic environment*<br><br>Economic<br>Political, fiscal, legal<br>Social, cultural<br>Technological<br>Intra-company<br><br>*The market*<br><br>Total market, size, growth and trends (value/volume)<br>Market characteristics, developments and trends: products, prices, physical distribution, channels, customers/ | consumers, communication, industry practices<br><br>*Competition*<br><br>Major competitors<br>Size<br>Market shares coverage<br>Market standing and reputation<br>Production capabilities<br>Distribution policies<br>Marketing methods<br>Extent of diversification<br>Personnel issues<br>International links<br>Profitability<br>Key strengths and weaknesses | *Own company*<br><br>Sales (total by geographical location, by industrial type, by customer, by product)<br>Market shares<br>Profit margins, costs<br>Marketing information, research<br>Marketing mix variables, product management, price, distribution, promotion, operations and resources |

which should be investigated under both headings. Each should be examined with a view to building up an information base relevant to the company's performance.

Many people mistakenly believe that the marketing audit should be some kind of final attempt to define a company's marketing problem, or at best something done by an independent body from time to time to ensure that a company is on the right track. However, many highly successful companies, as well as using normal information and control procedures and marketing research throughout the year, start their planning cycle each year with a formal, audit-type process, covering everything that has had an important influence on marketing activities. Certainly in many leading consumer goods companies the annual self-audit approach is a tried-and-tested discipline.

Occasionally it may be justified for outside consultants to carry out the audit in order to check that the company is getting the most out of its resources. However, it seems an unnecessary expense to have this done every year.

Objections to line managers doing their own audits usually centre around the problem of time and objectivity. In practice a disciplined approach and thorough training will help. But the discipline must be applied from the highest to the lowest levels of management if the tunnel vision that often results from a lack of critical appraisal is to be avoided.

The next question is: what happens to the results of the audit? Some companies consume valuable resources carrying out audits that produce very little in the way of results. The audit is simply a database, and the task remains of turning it into intelligence, that is information essential to decision-making.

It is often helpful to adopt a regular format for the major findings. One way of doing this is in the form of a SWOT analysis. Table 5.1 gives a summary of the audit under the headings of internal strengths and weaknesses as they relate to external opportunities and threats.

The SWOT analysis should, if possible, contain no more than four or five pages of commentary, focusing only on key factors. It should highlight internal strengths and weaknesses measured against the competition's, and key external opportunities and threats. A summary of reasons for good or bad performance should be included. It should be interesting to read, contain concise statements, include only relevant and important data and give greater emphasis to creative analysis.

Having completed the marketing audit and SWOT analysis,

fundamental assumptions on future conditions have to be made explicit. An example of an explicit assumption might be: 'With respect to the company's industrial climate, it is assumed that industrial overcapacity will increase from 105 per cent to 115 per cent as new industrial plants come into operation; price competition will force price levels down by 10 per cent across the board; a new product will be introduced by our major competitor before the end of the second quarter.' Assumptions should be few in number. If a plan is viable irrespective of the assumptions made, then the assumptions are unnecessary.

The next step is the writing of marketing objectives and strategies. An objective is what you want to achieve, a strategy is how you plan to achieve it. This is the key to the whole process and undoubtedly the most important and difficult of all stages. If this is not done properly, everything that follows is of little value.

It is an obvious activity to follow on with, since a thorough review, particularly of its markets, should enable the company to determine whether it will be able to meet the long-range financial targets with its current range of products. Any projected gap has to be filled by new product development or market extension.

It should be emphasized that this is the stage in the planning cycle at which a compromise has to be reached between what is wanted by various departments and what is practicable, given all the constraints upon the company. At this stage, objectives and strategies should be set for five years ahead, or for whatever the planning horizon is.

The important point to remember about marketing objectives is that they are concerned solely with products and markets. Common sense will confirm that it is only by selling something to someone that the company's financial goals can be achieved; pricing and service levels are the means by which the goals are achieved. Thus pricing, sales promotion and advertising objectives should not be confused with marketing objectives. The latter are concerned with one or more of the following:

- existing products in existing markets
- new products for existing markets
- existing products for new markets
- new products for new markets.

They should be capable of measurement, otherwise, they are not worthwhile. Directional terms, such as 'maximize', 'minimize', 'penetrate' and 'increase', are only acceptable if quantitative measurement can be attached to them. Measurement should be in terms of sales volume, value, market share, percentage penetration of outlets, and so on.

Marketing strategies, the means by which the objectives will be achieved, are generally concerned with the 'four P's':

- Product: deletions, modifications, additions, design, packaging, and so on.
- Price: policies to be followed for product groups in market segments.
- Place: distribution channels and customer service levels.
- Promotion: communicating with customers under the relevant headings, ie. advertising, sales force, sales promotion, public relations, exhibitions, direct mail, and so on.

The following list of marketing strategies (in summary form), cover the majority of options open under the headings of the four P's:

- Product
  - expand the line
  - change performance, quality or features
  - consolidate the line
  - standardize design
  - positioning
  - change the mix
  - branding.
- Price
  - change price, terms or conditions
  - skimming policies
  - penetration policies.
- Promotion
  - change advertising or promotion
  - change selling.
- Place
  - change delivery or distribution
  - change service
  - change channels
  - change the degree of forward integration.

Having completed this major planning task, it is normal at this stage to employ judgement, experience, field tests, and so on, to test out the feasibility of the objectives and strategies in terms of market share, sales, costs and profits. It is also at this stage that alternative plans and mixes are normally considered.

General marketing strategies should now be reduced to specific objectives, each supported by more detailed strategy and action statements. A company organized according to functions might have an advertising plan, a sales promotion plan and a pricing plan. A product-based company might have a product plan, with objectives, strategies and tactics for price, place and promotion, as required. A market-based or geographically based company might have a market plan, with objectives, strategies and tactics for the four P's, as required. Likewise, a company with a few major customers might have a customer plan. Any combination of the above might be suitable, depending on circumstances.

There is a clear distinction between strategy and detailed implementation or tactics. Marketing strategy reflects the company's best opinion as to how it can most profitably apply its skills and resources to the market-place. It is inevitably broad in scope. The plan which stems from it will spell out action and timings and will contain the detailed contribution expected from each department.

There is a similarity between strategy in business and strategic military development. One looks at the enemy, the terrain, the resources under command and then decides whether to attack the whole front, an area of enemy weakness, to feint in one direction while attacking in another, or to attempt an encirclement of the enemy's position. The policy and mix, the type of tactics to be used and the criteria for judging success, all come under the heading of strategy. The action steps are tactics. Similarly, in marketing, the same commitment, mix and type of resources as well as tactical guidelines and criteria that must be met, all come under the heading of strategy. For example, the decision to use distributors in all but the three largest market areas, in which company salesmen will be used, is a strategic decision. The selection of particular distributors is a tactical decision.

Formulating marketing strategies is one of the most critical and difficult parts of the entire marketing process. It sets the limit of success. Communicated to all management levels, it indicates what strengths are to be developed, what weaknesses are to be remedied, and in what manner. Marketing strategies enable operating decisions to bring the company into the right relationship with the emerging pattern of market opportunities which previous analysis has shown to offer the highest prospect of success.

A written strategic marketing plan is the backdrop against which operational decisions are taken. Consequently too much detail should be avoided. Its major function is to determine where the company is, where it wants to go and how it can get there. It lies at the heart of a company's revenue-generating activities, such as the timing of the cash flow and the size and character of the labour force. What should actually appear in a written strategic marketing plan is shown below.

1 Start with a market overview:
   ■ Has the market declined or grown?
   ■ How does it break down into segments?
   ■ What is your share of each?
   Keep it simple. If you do have the facts, make estimates. Use life-cycles, portfolios, bar charts and pie charts and make it all crystal clear.
2 Now identify the key segments and do a SWOT for each one:
   ■ Outline the major external influences and their impact on each segment.
   ■ List the key factors for success
   ■ Give an assessment of the company's differential strengths and weaknesses compared with those of its competitors.
   ■ Give an explanation for good or bad performance.
3 Specify the major assumptions on which the plan is based.
4 Set objectives and delineate the major strategies under each of the four P's.
5 State the financial consequences in the form of a budget.

The strategic marketing plan should be distributed only to those who need it, but it can only be an aid to effective management. It cannot be a substitute for it.

It will be obvious from all of this that not only does budget setting become much easier and more realistic, but the resulting budgets are more likely to reflect what the whole company wants to achieve, rather than just one department.

The problem of designing a dynamic system for setting budgets is a major challenge to the marketing and financial directors of all companies. The most satisfactory approach would be for a marketing director to justify all marketing expenditure from a zero base each year against the tasks to be accomplished. If these procedures are followed, a hierarchy of objectives is built up in such a way that every item of budgeted expenditure can be related directly back to the initial financial objectives. For example, if sales promotion is an important means of achieving an objective, when a sales promotion item appears in the programme it has a specific purpose which can be related back to a major objective. Thus every item of expenditure is fully accounted for.

Marketing expense can be considered to be all costs that are incurred after the product leaves the factory, apart from those involved in physical distribution. When it comes to pricing, any form of discounting that reduces the expected gross income – such as promotional or quantity discounts, overriders, sales commission and unpaid invoices – should be given the most careful attention as marketing expenses. Most obvious marketing expenses will occur, however, under the heading of promotion, in the form of advertising, sales salaries and expenses, sales promotion and direct mail costs.

The important point about the measurable effects of marketing activity is that anticipated levels should result from careful analysis of what is required to take the company towards its goals, while the most careful attention should be paid to gathering all items of expenditure under appropriate headings. The healthiest way of treating these issues is through zero-based budgeting.

In the last section in this chapter the planning process is put into the context of different kinds of organizational structures, and the design and implementation of systems are described.

## Marketing planning systems design and implementation

In this final section we look at some of the *contextual* issues of strategic marketing planning. The truth is, of course, that the actual *process* of marketing planning is simple in outline. Marketing text books will tell us that it consists of a situation review, assumptions, objectives, strategies, programmes and measurement and review. What the books *do not* tell us is that there are a number of contextual issues that have to be considered that make marketing planning one of the most substantial of all management problems.

Here are some of those issues:

- When should it be done, how often, by whom, and how?
- Is it different in a large and a small company?
- Is it different in a diversified and an undiversified company?
- What is the role of the chief executive?
- What is the role of the planning department?
- Should marketing planning be top-down or bottom-up?
- What is the relationship between operational (one year) and strategic (longer term) planning?

### *Requisite strategic marketing planning*

Many companies currently under siege have recognized the need for a more structured approach to planning their marketing and have opted for the kind of standardized, formalized procedures written about so much in textbooks. These rarely bring any benefits and often bring marketing planning itself into disrepute.

It is quite clear that any attempt at the introduction of formalized marketing planning systems has serious organizational and behavioural implications for any company, as it requires a change in its approach to managing its business. It is also clear that unless a company recognizes these implications, and plans to seek ways of coping with them, formalized strategic planning will be ineffective.

Our research has indicated that the implications of the introduction of formal marketing planning systems are principally as follows:

- Any closed-loop planning system (but especially one that is essentially a forecasting and budgeting system) will lead to uninspired and ineffective marketing. Therefore there has to be some mechanism for preventing inertia from setting in through the over-bureaucratization of the system.
- Planning undertaken at the functional level of marketing, in the absence of a means of integration with other functional areas of the business at general-management level, will be largely ineffective.
- The separation of responsibility for operational and strategic planning will lead to a divergence of the short-term thrust of a business at the operational level from the long-term objectives of the enterprise as a whole. This will encourage a preoccupation with short-term results at operational level, which normally makes the firm less effective in the long term.
- Unless the chief executive understands and takes an active role in strategic marketing planning, it will never be an effective system.
- A period of up to three years is necessary (especially in large firms) for the successful introduction of an effective strategic planning system.

Let us be dogmatic about requisite planning levels. First, in a large diversified group, irrespective of such organizational issues, anything other than a systematic approach approximating to a formalized marketing planning system is unlikely to enable the necessary control to be exercised over the corporate identity. Second, unnecessary planning, or overplanning, could easily result from an inadequate or indiscriminate consideration of the real planning needs at the different levels in the hierarchical chain. Third, as size and diversity grow, so the degree of formalization of

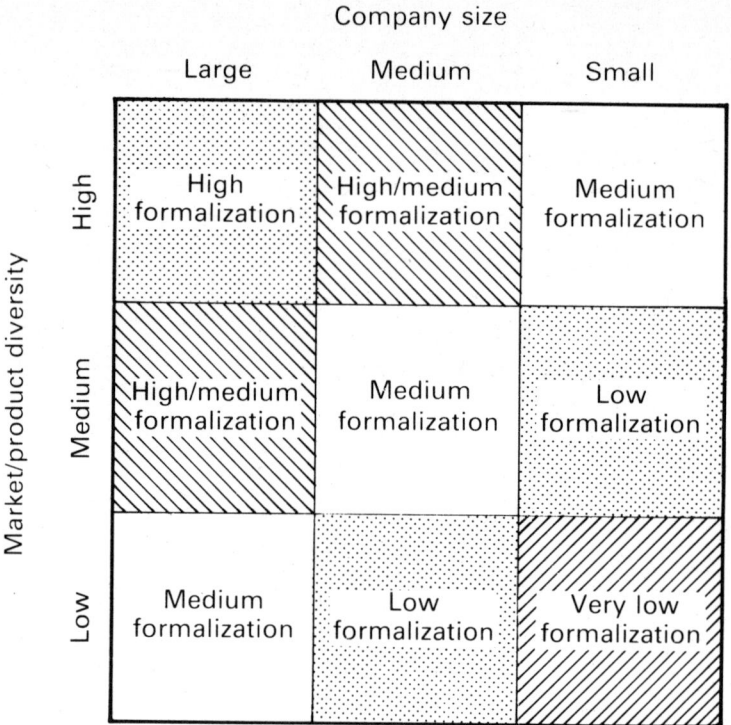

**Figure 5.4   Influences on the planning process**

the marketing planning process must also increase. This can be simplified in the form of a matrix (Figure 5.4).

The degree of formalization must increase with the evolving size and diversity of operations. However, while the degree of formalization will change, the need for an effective marketing planning system does not. The problems that companies suffer, then, are a function of either the degree to which they have a requisite marketing planning system or the degree to which the formalization of their system grows with the situational complexities attendant upon the size and diversity of operations.

Figure 5.5 explores four key outcomes that marketing planning can evoke. It can be seen that systems I, III and IV – that is, (I) where the individual is totally subordinate to a formalized system, or (III) where individuals are allowed to do what they want without any system, or (IV) where there is neither system nor creativity – are less successful than system II, in which the individual is allowed

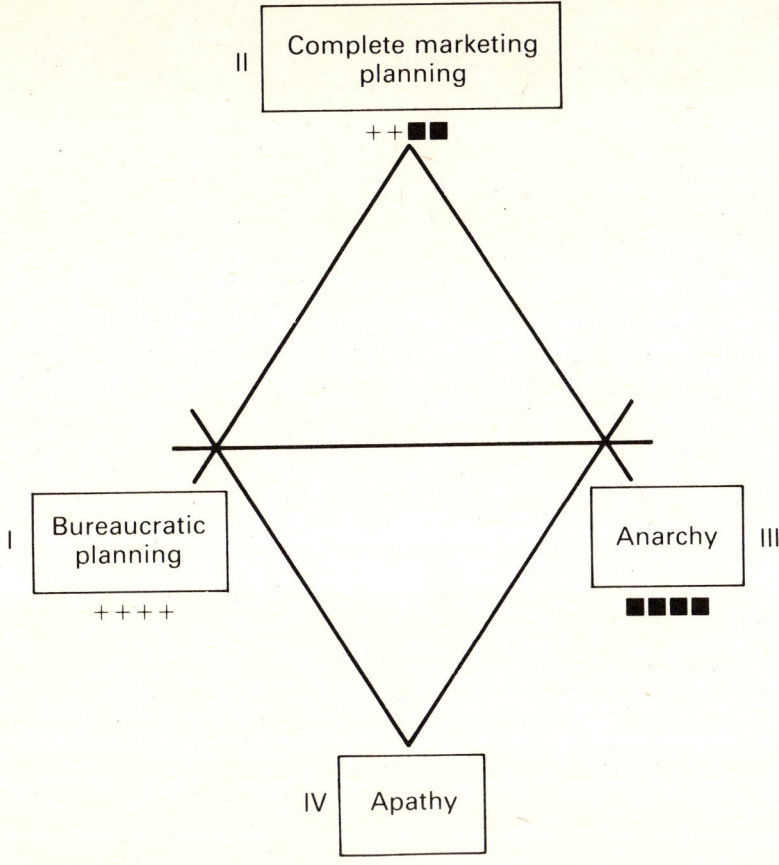

+ Degree of formalization
■ Degree of openness

**Figure 5.5   Four possible outcomes of marketing planning**

to be entrepreneurial within a total system. System II, then, will be an effective marketing planning system, but one in which the degree of formalization will be a function of company size and diversity.

Creativity cannot flourish in a closed-loop formalized system. There would be little disagreement that in today's abrasive, turbulent and highly competitive environment it is those firms that succeed in extracting entrepreneurial ideas and creative marketing programmes from systems that are necessarily yet acceptably formalized, that will succeed in the long run. Innovative flair can so easily get stifled by systems. Certainly there is ample evidence of international companies with highly formalized systems that produce stale and repetitive plans, with few changes from year to year and that fail to point up the really key strategic issues as a result. There is clearly a need, therefore, to find a way of perpetually renewing the planning life-cycle each time around. Inertia must never set in. Without some such valve or means of opening up the loop, inertia quickly produces decay.

Such a valve has to be inserted early in the planning cycle during the audit, or situation-review stage. In companies with effective strategic marketing planning systems, whether such systems are formalized or informal, the critical intervention of senior managers, from the chief executive down through the hierarchical chain, comes at the audit stage. Essentially what takes place is a personalized presentation of audit findings, together with proposed marketing objectives and strategies and outline budgets for the strategic planning period. These are discussed, amended where necessary and agreed in various synthesized formats at the hierarchical levels in the organisation *before* any detailed operational planning takes place. It is at such meetings that managers are called upon to justify their views, which tends to force them to be more bold and creative than they would have been had they been allowed merely to send in their proposals. Obviously, however, even here much depends on the degree to which managers take a critical stance, which is much greater when the chief executive himself takes an active part in the process. Every hour of time devoted at this stage by the chief executive has a multiplier effect throughout the remainder of the process. And let it be remembered, we are not talking about budgets at this juncture in anything other than outline form.

## Overview

Marketing planning is not to be confused with budgets and forecasts. Rather, marketing planning is the way companies can identify what is selling and to whom.

The external environment today is increasingly complex, with static or even declining markets the norm. Old methods of planning and doing business no longer work; a new, disciplined and systematic approach to the market must be developed to take the company from operational to strategic modes.

This entails scanning the external environment, identifying the forces emanating from it and creating the appropriate strategic responses. A three-part logic is described which can help organizations build a strategic marketing capability.

The process itself contains nine key elements: corporate objectives, marketing audit, SWOT analysis, assumptions, marketing objectives and strategies, estimation of expected results, alternatives and mixes, programmes, measurements and results. A feedback loop ensures that our assumptions concur with our results.

While these steps are discussed in detail, the chapter concludes that any effective marketing planning process must take into account the different kinds of organizational structures and contextual issues which result. A standardized, textbook approach can often bring marketing planning into disrepute. Companies should strive to understand and work with the implications and influences inherent in marketing planning.

# 6 Strategic analysis

Before examining specific tools and techniques it would be useful to begin by discussing the relationship between strategic marketing planning and corporate planning. There are five steps in the corporate planning process. As can be seen from Figure 6.1, the starting point should be a statement of corporate financial objectives for the long-range planning period of the company, which are often expressed in terms of turnover, profit before tax and return on investment.

More often than not, this long-range planning horizon is five years, but the precise period should be determined by the nature of the markets in which the company operates. For example, five years would not be a long enough period for a glass manufacturer, since it takes that period of time to commission a new furnace, whereas in some fashion industries five years would be too long. A useful guideline in determining the planning horizon is that there should be a market for the company products for long enough at least to amortize any capital investment associated with those products.

Step 2 is the *management audit*. This is important since a thorough situation review, particularly in the area of marketing, should enable the company to determine whether it will be able to meet the long-range financial targets with its current range of products in its current markets.

Undoubtedly the most important and difficult of all stages in the corporate planning process is Step 3, *objective and strategy setting*, since if this is not done properly, everything that follows is of little value.

The important point to make is that this is the time in the planning cycle when a compromise has to be reached between what is desired and what is practicable, given all the constraints that any company has. For example, it is no good setting a marketing objective of penetrating a new market if the company does not have the

| Step 1 Corporate financial objectives | Step 2 Management audit | Step 3 Objective and strategy setting | Step 4 Plans | Step 5 Corporate plans |
|---|---|---|---|---|
| | *Marketing audit* Marketing | Marketing objectives, strategies | Marketing plan | |
| | *Distribution audit* Stocks and control; transportation; warehousing | Distribution objectives, strategies | Distribution plan | Issue of corporate plan, to include corporate objectives and strategies; production objectives and strategies, etc.; long-range profit-and-loss accounts; balance sheets |
| | *Production audit* Value analysis; engineering development; work study; quality control; labour; materials, plant and space utilization; production planning; factories | Production objectives, strategies | Production plan | |
| | *Financial audit* Credit, debt, cash-flow and budgetary control; resource allocation; capital expenditure; long-term finance | Financial objectives, strategies | Financial plan | |
| | *Personnel audit* Management, technical and administrative ability, etc. | Personnel objectives, strategies | | |

**Figure 6.1   Strategic marketing planning and its place in the corporate planning cycle**

production capacity to cope with the new business and if capital is not available for whatever investment is necessary in additional capacity. At this stage, objectives and strategies will be set for five years, or for whatever the planning horizon is.

Step 4 involves producing detailed *plans* for one year, containing the responsibilities, timing and costs of carrying out the first year's objectives, and broad plans for the following years.

These plans can then be incorporated into the *corporate plan* (Step 5), which will contain long-range corporate objectives, strategies, plans, profit-and-loss accounts and balance sheets. Such a corporate plan, being the result of the process described above, is more likely to provide long-term stability for a company than plans based on a more intuitive process and containing forecasts which tend to be little more than extrapolations of previous trends.

The headquarters of one multinational company with a sophisticated budgeting system used to receive 'plans' from all over the world and co-ordinate them in quantitative and cross-functional terms such as numbers of employees, units of sale, items of plant, square feet of production area, and so on, together with the associated financial implications. The trouble was that the whole complicated edifice was built on the initial sales forecasts, which were themselves little more than a time-consuming numbers game. The really key strategic issues relating to products and markets were lost in all the financial activity, which eventually resulted in grave operational and profitability problems.

What is a corporate objective and what is a marketing objective? An objective is what you want to achieve. A strategy is how you plan to achieve your objectives. An objective will ensure that a company knows what its strategies are expected to accomplish and when a particular strategy has accomplished its purpose. In other words, without objectives, strategy decisions and all that follows will take place in a vacuum.

Following the identification of opportunities and the explicit statement of assumptions about conditions affecting the business, the process of setting objectives in theory should be comparatively easy, the actual objectives themselves being a realistic statement of what the company desires to achieve as a result of a market-centred analysis rather than generalized statements born of top management's desire to 'do better next year'. However, objective setting is more complex than at first it would appear to be.

Most experts agree that the logical approach to the difficult task of setting marketing objectives is to proceed from the broad to the specific. Thus the starting point would be a statement of the nature of the business, from which would flow the broad company objectives. Next the broad company objectives would be translated into key result areas, which would be those areas in which success is vital to the firm. Market penetration, and growth rate of sales, are examples of key result areas. The third step would be creation of the sub-objectives necessary to accomplish the broad objectives, such as sales-volume goals, geographical expansion, product-line extension, and so on.

The end result of this process should be objectives which are consistent with the strategic plan, attainable within budget limitations and compatible with the strengths, limitations and economics of other functions within the organization.

At the top level, management is concerned with long-run profitability; at the next level in the management hierarchy the concern is for objectives which are defined more specifically and in greater detail, such as increasing sales and market share, obtaining new markets, and so on. These objectives are merely a part of the hierarchy of objectives, in that corporate objectives will only be accomplished if these and other objectives are achieved. At the next level, management is concerned with objectives which are defined even more tightly, such as: to create awareness among a specific target market about a new product; to change a particular customer attitude; and so on. Again, the general marketing objectives will only be accomplished if these and other sub-objectives are achieved. It is clear that sub-objectives *per se*, unless they are an integral part of a broader framework of objectives, are likely to lead to a wasteful misdirection of resources.

For example, a sales increase in itself may be possible, but only at an undue cost, so that such a marketing objective is only appropriate within the framework of corporate objectives. In such a case it may well be that an increase in sales in a particular market sector will entail additional capital expenditure ahead of the time for which it is planned. If this were the case, it may make more sense to allocate available production capacity to more profitable market sectors in the short term, allowing sales to decline in another sector. Decisions such as this are likely to be more easily made against a backcloth of explicitly stated broad company objectives relating to all the major disciplines.

Likewise, objectives should be set for advertising, for example, which are wholly consistent with wider objectives. Objectives set in this way integrate the advertising effort with the other elements in the marketing mix, and this leads to a consistent, logical marketing plan.

Corporate objectives and strategies can be simplified in the following way:

- Corporate objective – desired level of profitability

- Corporate strategies – which products and which markets (marketing)
  - what kind of facilities (production and distribution)
  - size and character of the staff/ labour force (personnel)
  - funding (finance)
  - other corporate strategies such as social responsibility, corporate image, stock-market image, employee image, and so on.

It is now clear that at the next level down in the organization, that is the functional level, what products are to be sold into what markets, become *marketing objectives*, while the means of achieving these objectives using the marketing mix, are *marketing strategies*. At the next level down there would be, say, *advertising objectives* and *advertising strategies*, with the subsequent *programmes* and *budgets* for achieving the objectives. In this way, a hierarchy of objectives and strategies can be traced back to the initial corporate objective. Figure 6.2 illustrates this point.

## Tools and techniques for strategic analysis

There are a number of basic concepts of specific relevance for chief executives and directors, in the process of setting marketing objectives and in formulating strategies for products, prices, distribution and promotion.

However, since much of this chapter is about products, it is important to start by defining exactly what is meant by the term 'product'. There are three definitions, each with its own distinct meaning, depending on the level of aggregation involved:

- *Product class* means all products of all competing producers which essentially serve a set of functional needs in approximately the same manner. For instance, carpets can be defined as a product class since they all satisfy the need for comfort and colour in respect of floorcovering.
- *Product sub-class* means homogeneous groupings of products within a product class, as perceived by the user. For example, luxury cars, sports cars, personal computers and pure wool carpets are all examples of product sub-classes.

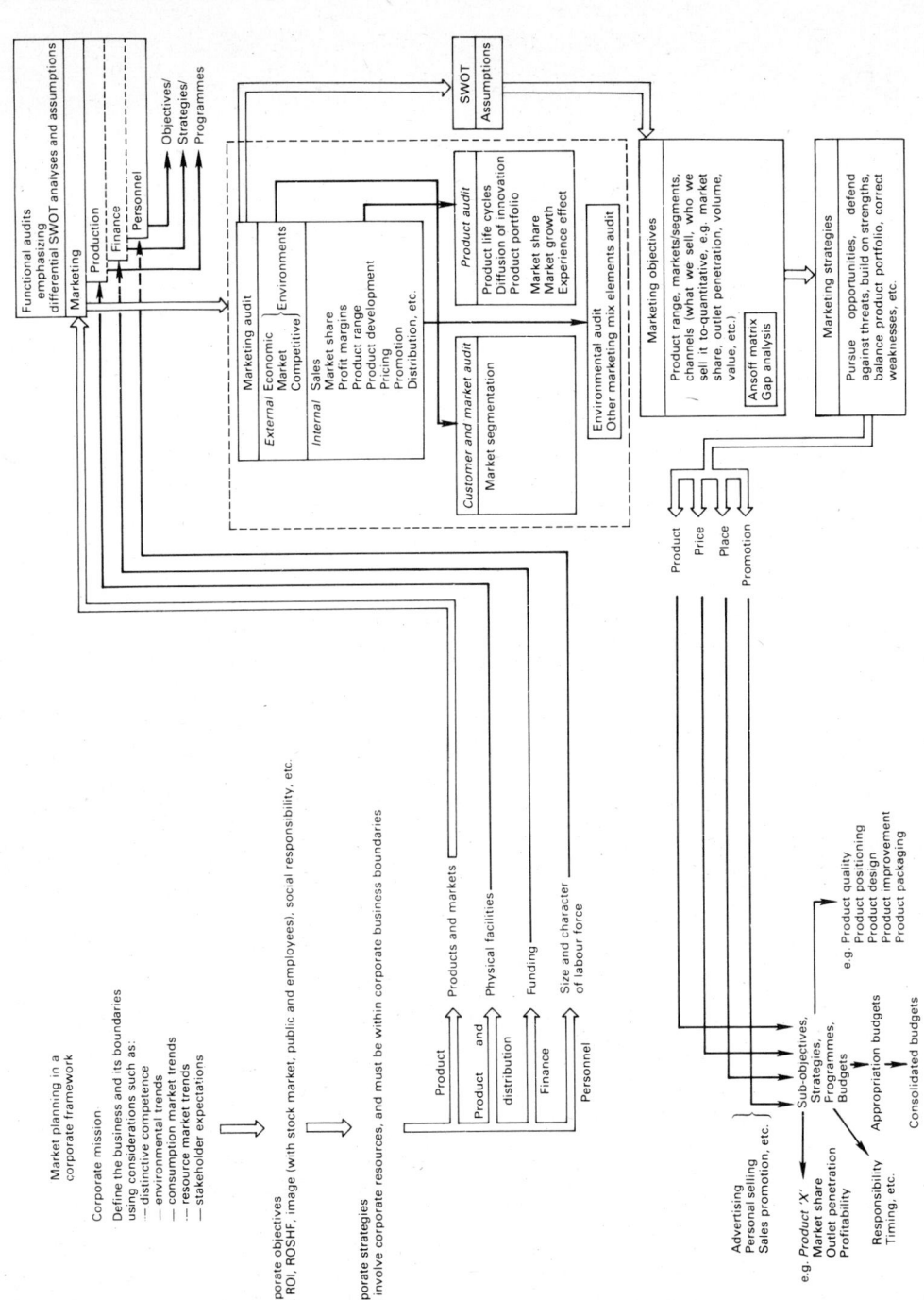

**Figure 6.2 Marketing planning in a corporate context**

- *Brand* is a term used to describe specific products in a sub-class, such as Jaguar, Mars Bar, Marlboro, and so on.

## How to set market objectives

The Ansoff matrix (named after its originator, Professor Igor Ansoff) can now be introduced as a useful tool to aid in the search for appropriate marketing objectives. The competitive context of the business can be simplified to two dimensions only – products and markets. To put it even more simply, Ansoff's framework is about what is sold (the 'product') and who it is sold to (the 'market'). The matrix in Figure 6.3 depicts these concepts.

It is clear that the range of possible marketing objectives is very wide, since there will be degrees of technological 'newness' and degrees of market 'newness'. Nevertheless, Ansoff's matrix provides a logical framework in which marketing objectives can be developed under each of the four main headings. Common sense will confirm that it is only by selling something to someone that the company's financial goals can be achieved, and that advertising, pricing, service levels, and so on, are the means (or strategies) by

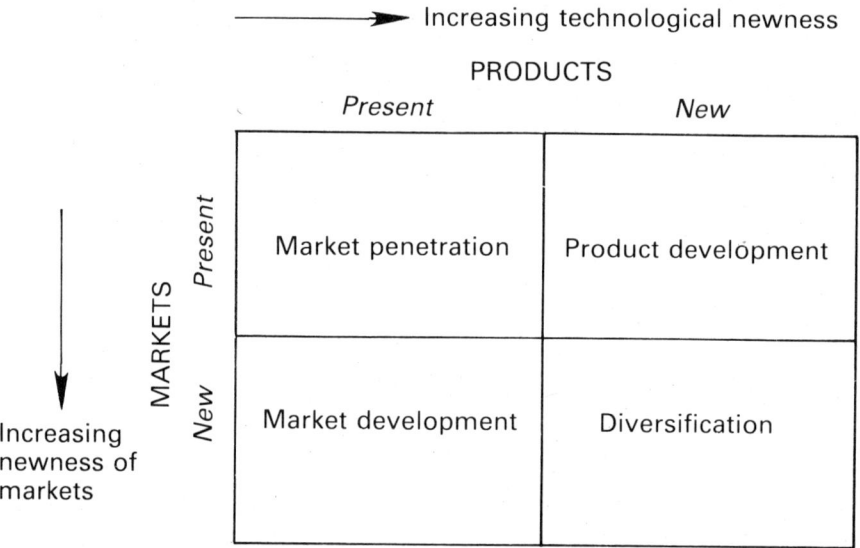

**Figure 6.3   Ansoff matrix**

which it might succeed in doing this. Thus pricing objectives, sales promotion objectives, advertising objectives, and the like, should not be confused with marketing objectives.

Marketing objectives are generally accepted as being selected qualitative and quantitative commitments, usually stated either in terms of standards of performance for a given operating period, or conditions to be achieved by given dates. Performance standards are usually stated in terms of sales volume and various measures of profitability. The conditions to be attained are usually a percentage of market share and various other commitments, such as a percentage of the total number of a given type of retail outlet.

There is also broad agreement that objectives must be specific enough to enable subordinates to derive from them the general character of action required and the yardstick by which performance is to be judged. Objectives are the core of managerial action, providing direction to the plans. By asking where the operation should be at some future date, objectives are determined. Vague objectives, however emotionally appealing, are counter-productive to sensible planning, and are usually the result of the human propensity for wishful thinking, which often smacks more of cheerleading than serious marketing leadership. What this really means is that it is arguable whether directional terms such as 'decrease', 'optimize', 'minimize' should be used as objectives; it seems logical that unless there is some measure, or yardstick, against which to measure a sense of movement towards achieving them, then they do not serve any useful purpose.

Ansoff defines an objective as, 'a measure of the efficiency of the resource-conversion process. An objective contains three elements: the particular attribute that is chosen as a measure of efficiency; the yardstick or scale by which the attribute is measured; and the particular value on the scale which the firm seeks to attain.'

Marketing objectives, then, are about each of the four main categories of the Ansoff matrix:

- existing products in existing markets – these may be many and varied and will certainly need to be set for all existing major products and customer groups (segments)
- new products in existing markets
- existing products in new markets
- new products in new markets.

Simply defined, product/market strategy means the route chosen to achieve company goals through the range of products it offers to its chosen market segments. Thus the product/market strategy

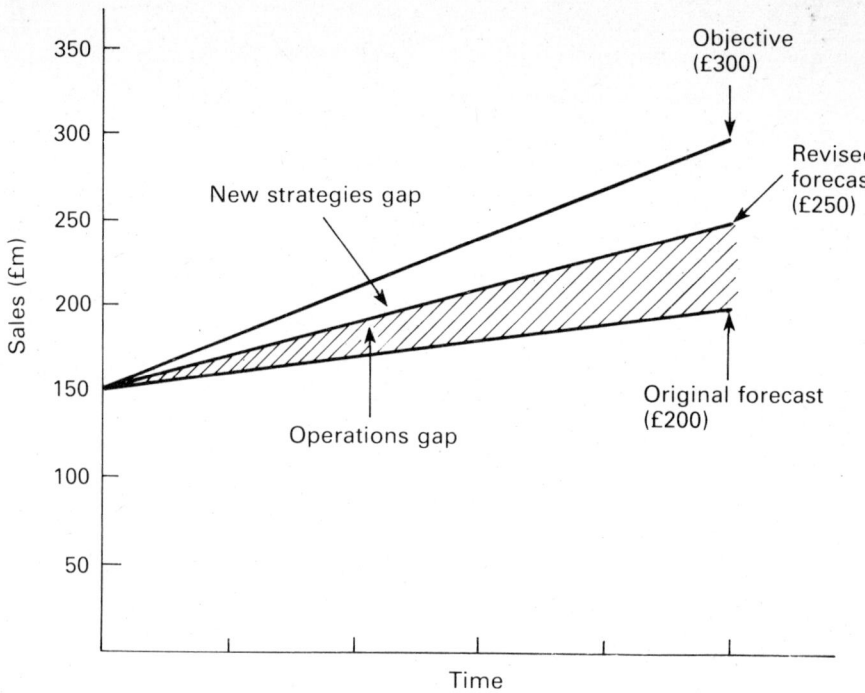

**Figure 6.4   The strategic gap**

represents a commitment to a future direction for the firm. Marketing objectives, then, are concerned solely with products and markets.

Figure 6.4 illustrates what is commonly referred to as 'strategic gap'. Essentially what it suggests is that if the corporate sales and financial objectives are greater than the current long-range forecasts, there is a gap which has to be filled. In practice it is sensible to recognize two 'gaps': an operations gap and a new strategies gap.

The operations gap can be filled in two ways:

- improved productivity, for example reduce costs, improve the sales mix, increase prices
- market penetration, for example increase usage, increase market share.

The new strategies gap can be filled in four ways:

- reduce objectives
- market development, for example find new user groups, enter new segments, geographical expansion

- product development
- diversification, for example selling new products to new markets.

If improved productivity is one method by which the expansion gap is to be filled, care must be taken not to take measures such as to reduce marketing costs by 20 per cent overall. Portfolio analysis, which will be discussed later in the chapter, will indicate that this would be totally inappropriate to some product/market areas, for which increased marketing expenditure may be needed, while for others 20 per cent reduction in marketing costs may not be sufficient.

As for the other options, it is clear that market penetration should always be a company's first option, since it makes far more sense to attempt to increase profits and cash flow from *existing* products and markets initially, because this is usually the least costly and the least risky. This is so because for its present products and markets a company has developed knowledge and skills which it can use competitively (asset-based marketing).

For the same reason, it makes more sense in many cases to move along the horizontal axis for further growth before attempting to find new markets. The reason for this is that it normally takes many years for a company to get to know its customers and markets and to build up a reputation. That reputation and trust, embodied in either the company's name or in its brands, is rarely transferable to new markets, where other companies are already entrenched.

The marketing audit should ensure that the method chosen to fill the gap is consistent with the company's capabilities and builds on its strengths. For example, it would normally prove far less profitable for a dry goods grocery manufacturer to introduce frozen foods than to add another dry foods product. Likewise, if a product could be sold to existing channels using the existing sales force, this is far less risky than introducing a new product that requires new channels and new selling skills.

Exactly the same applies to the company's production, distribution and people. Whatever new products are developed should be as consistent as possible with the company's known strengths and capabilities. Clearly the use of existing plant capacity is generally preferable to new processes. Also, the amount of additional investment is important. Technical personnel are highly trained and specialist, and whether this competence can be transferred to a new field must be considered. A product requiring new raw materials may also require new handling and storage techniques, which may prove expensive.

It can now be appreciated why going into new markets with new products (diversification) is the riskiest strategy of all, because *new* resources and *new* management skills have to be developed. This is why the history of business is replete with examples of companies which went bankrupt through moving into areas where they had little or no distinctive competence. This is also why many companies that diversified through acquisition during periods of high economic growth have since divested themselves of businesses that were not basically compatible with their own distinctive competence.

The Ansoff matrix, of course, is not a simple four-box matrix, for it will be obvious that there are degrees of technological newness as well as degrees of market newness. Figure 6.5 illustrates the point. It also demonstrates more easily why any movement should generally aim to keep a company as close as possible to its present position rather than moving it to a totally unrelated position, except in the most unusual circumstances.

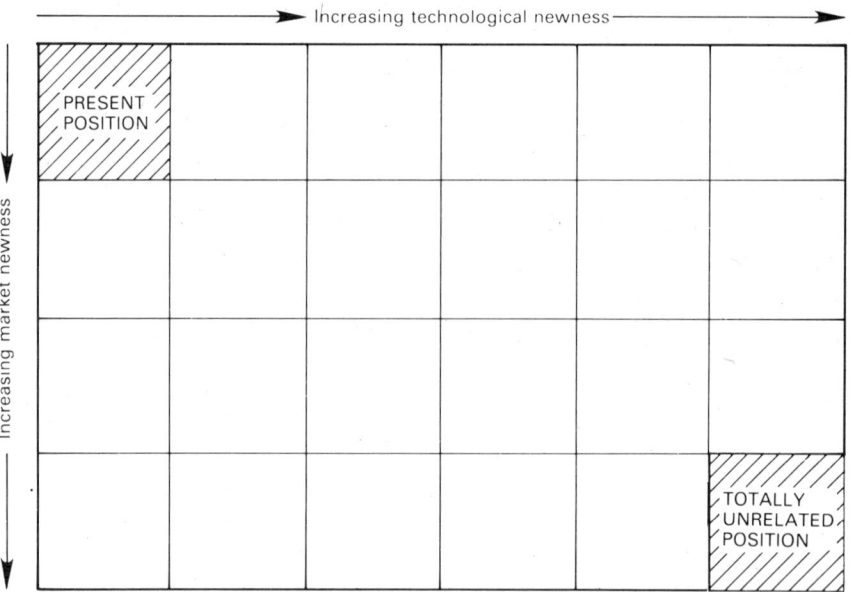

**Figure 6.5   The dimensions of change**

Nevertheless, there are certain phenomena which will inevitably *force* companies to move along one or other of the Ansoff matrix axes if they are to continue to increase their sales and profits. We now turn our attention to what these phenomena are and will consider the product life-cycle as a valuable marketing tool before going on to discuss *how* decisions should be taken to move along the axes using portfolio management techniques.

## Product life-cycle analysis

There are many examples of entrepreneurs who set themselves up in business to manufacture, say, toys such as skateboards, who make their fortune and who then just as quickly lose it when this fashion-conscious market changes to its latest fad. Such examples are merely the extreme manifestation of what is known as the *product life-cycle*. This is such a vital and fundamental concept in marketing that it is worth devoting some time to a discussion of the subject.

Historians of technology have observed that all technical functions grow exponentially until they come up against some natural limiting factor which causes growth to slow down and eventually to decline as one technology is replaced by another. There is universal agreement that the same phenomenon applies to products, so giving rise to the concept of the product life-cycle, much written about in marketing literature during the past three decades.

The product life-cycle postulates that if a new product is successful at the introductory stage (and many fail at this point), then gradually repeat purchase grows and spreads and the rate of sales growth increases. At this stage competitors often enter the market and their additional promotional expenditures further

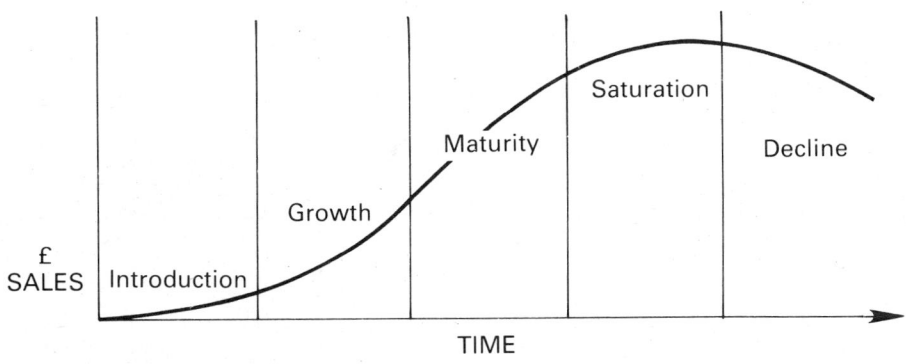

**Figure 6.6    The product life-cycle**

expand the market. But no market is infinitely expandable, and eventually the *rate* of growth slows as the product moves into its maturity stage. Eventually a point is reached where there are too many firms in the market, price wars break out, and some firms drop out of the market, until finally the market itself eventually falls into decline. Figure 6.6 illustrates these apparently universal phenomena.

However, problems occur with this useful generalization for one very important reason. Figure 6.7 illustrates the actual courses taken by a company in the management of one of its leading industrial products. As sales growth began to slow down, the company initiated a programme of product range extensions and market development which successfully took the brand into additional stages of growth. At the same time the company was aggressively seeking new products and even considering potential areas for diversification.

This clearly illustrates that because an individual producer can manipulate at will the amount of resources allocated to a particular

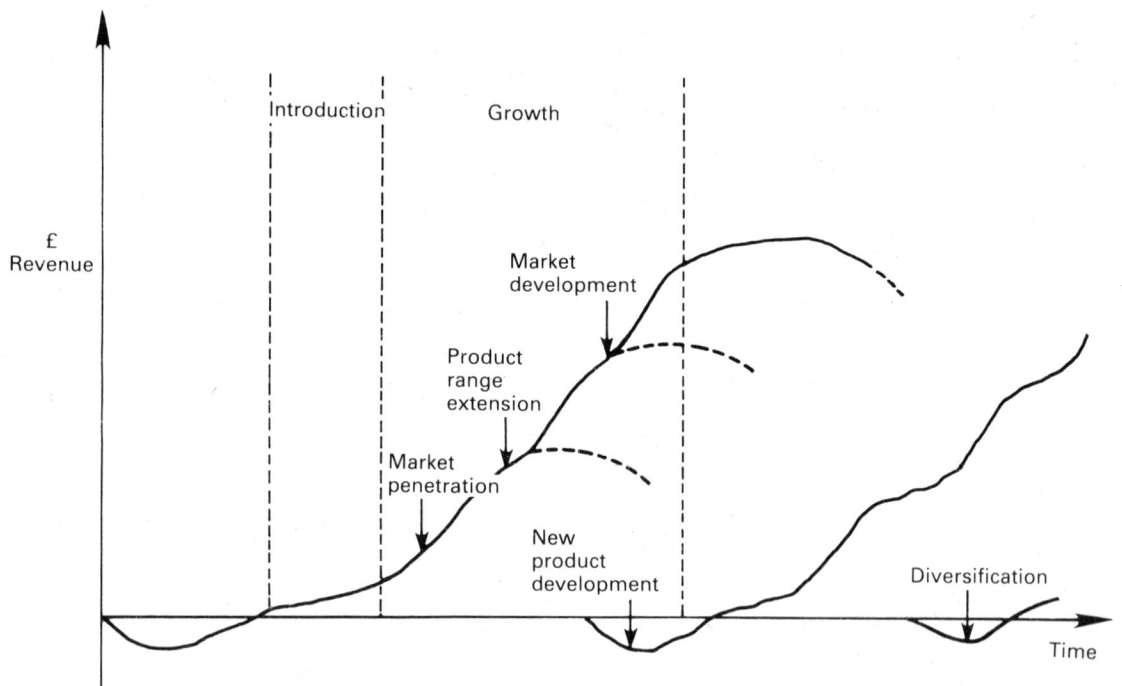

**Figure 6.7    The reality of the product life-cycle**

brand, plotting its sales in the manner of a life-cycle will give us very little insight into any underlying *market* behaviour. It will merely be a mirror image of a firm's resource allocation.

It is for this reason that *brand* life-cycle curves are, *per se*, of very little practical use if taken on their own. *Product class* and *product sub-class* life-cycle curves more commonly follow the classical shape. In particular, the product sub-class life-cycle can provide valuable insights, since marketing strategies are typically developed at this level. For instance, a company considering entering the personal computer business would gain more value from an analysis of the personal computer life-cycle than of that for computers as a whole, although the latter would clearly also be useful. At the product sub-class level, however, the two most common and interesting variables that interact with each other are market potential and the marketing strategy efforts of competitors. Market potential factors refer to the ability of the available population to absorb production of a given product sub-class per annum. In itself this is a function of a whole gamut of factors such as population size, the need for the product, the availability of suitable alternatives, income, prices, and so on.

The independent marketing strategies of all competitors operating in any product sub-class market obviously affect market size and market growth. Thus the two factors are interdependent and work together to provide the relatively consistent shapes of product life-cycle curves at the product-class and product sub-class levels.

From the strategic management point of view, the product life-cycle is useful in that it focuses our attention on what should be the appropriate strategies at different stages in the market development. Even more important are the implications of the product life-cycle concept for every element of the marketing mix. Figure 6.7 gives some guide as to how the product may have to change over its life-cycle. In addition to this, however, every other element also has to change. For example, if a company rigidly adhered to a premium pricing policy at the mature stage of the product life-cycle, when markets are often overcrowded and price wars begin, it could well lose market share. It could be regretted later on when the market has settled down, for it is often at this stage that products provide extremely profitable revenue for the company. It will become clearer later in this chapter why market share is important.

The same applies to promotion. During the early phase of product introduction, the task for advertising is usually one of creating awareness, whereas during the growth phase the task is likely to change to one of creating a favourable attitude towards the product. Neither should the policy towards channels be fixed. At first we are concerned with getting distribution for the product in the most important channels, whereas during the growth phase we have to consider ways of reaching the new channels that want our product.

The important point to remember at this stage is that the concept of the product life-cycle is not an academic figment of the imagination but a hard reality which is ignored at great risk. It is interesting to see how many commercial failures can be traced back to a naïve assumption on the part of managements that what was successful as a policy at one time will continue to be successful in the future.

Table 6.1 shows a checklist used by one major company to help it determine where its markets are on the life-cycle.

## Diffusion of innovation

A concept closely related to the product life-cycle is what is known as the 'diffusion of innovation' process. The diffusion of innovation refers to the cumulative percentage of potential adopters of a new product or service over time. Everett Rogers, an early researcher in this field, examined some of the social forces that explain the product life-cycle. The body of knowledge often referred to as 'reference theory' (which incorporates work on group norms, group pressures and the like), helps explain the snowball effect of diffusion. Rogers found that the actual rate of diffusion is a function of a product's

- relative advantage (over existing products)
- compatability (with life-styles, values, etc.)
- communicability (is it easy to communicate?)
- complexity (is it complicated?)
- divisibility (can it be tried out on a small scale before commitment?).

Diffusion is also a function of the newness of the product itself, which can be classified broadly under three headings:

- continuous innovation (e.g. the new miracle ingredient)
- dynamically continuous innovation (e.g. disposable lighter)
- discontinuous (e.g. microwave oven).

However, Rogers found that for all new products, not everyone

**Table 6.1**
**Guide to market maturity**

| Maturity stage Factor | Embryonic | Growth | Mature | Declining |
|---|---|---|---|---|
| 1 *Growth rate* | Normally much greater than GNP (on small base). | Sustained growth above GNP. New customers. New suppliers. Rate decelerates toward end of stage. | Approximately equals GNP. | Declining demand. Market shrinks as users' needs change. |
| 2 *Predictability of growth potential* | Hard to define accurately. Small portion of demand being satisfied. Market forecasts differ widely. | Greater percentage of demand is met and upper limits of demand becoming clearer. Discontinuities, such as price reductions based on economies of scale, may occur. | Potential well defined. Competition specialized to satisfy needs of specific segments. | Known and limited. |
| 3 *Product line proliferation* | Specialized lines to meet needs of early customers. | Rapid expansion. | Proliferation slows or ceases. | Lines narrow as unprofitable products dropped. |
| 4 *Number of competitors* | Unpredictable. | Reaches maximum. New entrants attracted by growth and high margins. Some consolidation begins toward end of stage. | Entrenched positions established. Further shakeout of marginal competitors. | New entrants unlikely. Competitors continue to decline. |

**Table 6.1** (*continued*)

| Maturity stage Factor | Embryonic | Growth | Mature | Declining |
|---|---|---|---|---|
| 5 *Market share distribution* | Unstable. Shares react unpredictably to entrepreneurial insights and timing. | Increasing stability. Typically, a few competitors emerging as strong. | Stable with a few companies often controlling much of industry. | Highly concentrated or fragmented as industry segments and/or is localized. |
| 6 *Customer stability* | Trial usage with little customer loyalty. | Some loyalty. Repeat usage with many seeking alternative suppliers. | Well-developed buying patterns with customer loyalty. Competitors understand purchase dynamics and it is difficult for a new supplier to win over accounts. | Extremely stable. Suppliers dwindle and customers less motivated to seek alternatives. |
| 7 *Ease of entry* | Normally easy. No one dominates. Customers' expectations uncertain. If barriers exist, they are usually technology, capital or fear of the unknown. | More difficult. Market franchises and/or economies of scale may exist, yet new business is still available without directly confronting competition. | Difficult. Market leaders established. New business must be 'won' from others. | Little or no incentive to enter. |

**Table 6.1** (*concluded*)

| Maturity stage Factor | Embryonic | Growth | Mature | Declining |
|---|---|---|---|---|
| 8 *Technology* | Plays an important role in matching product characteristics to market needs. Frequent product changes. | Product technology vital early, while process technology more important later in this stage. | Process and material substitution focus. Product requirements well known and relatively undemanding. May be a thrust to renew the industry via new technology. | Technological content is known, stable and accessible. |

adopts new products at the same time, and that a universal pattern emerged (Figure 6.8). In general the innovators think for themselves and try new things (where relevant); the early adopters, who have status in society, are opinion leaders and they adopt successful products, making them acceptable and respectable; the

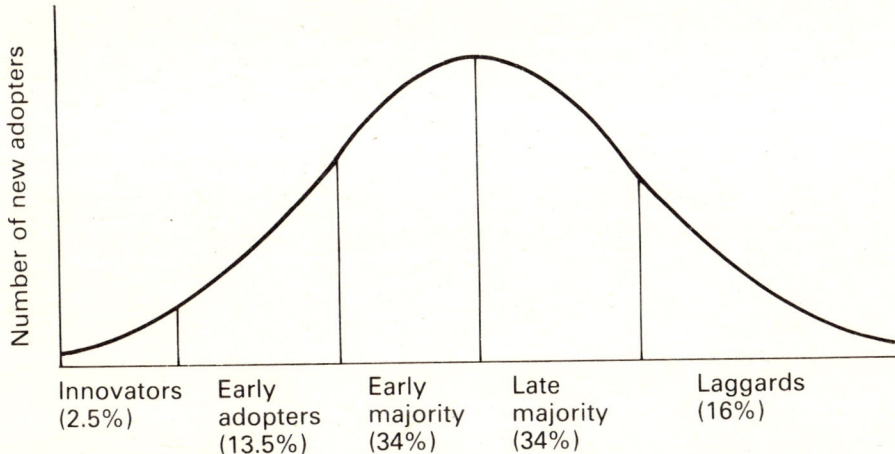

**Figure 6.8   The diffusion of innovations**

early majority, who are more conservative and who have slightly above-average status, are more deliberate and only adopt products that have social approbation; the late majority, who have below-average status and are more sceptical, adopt products much later; the laggards, with low status, income, and so on, view life through the rear mirror and are the last to adopt products.

This particular piece of research can be very useful, particularly for advertising and personal selling. For example, if we can develop a typology for innovative customers, we can target our early advertising and sales effort specifically at them. Once the first 3 per cent of innovators have adopted our product, there is a good chance that the early adopters will try it, and once the 10–12 per cent point is reached, the champagne can be opened, because there is a good chance that the rest will adopt our product.

We know, for example, that the *general* characteristics of opinion leaders are that they are venturesome, socially integrated, cosmopolitan, socially mobile and privileged. So we need to ask ourselves what are the *specific* characteristics of these customers in our particular industry. We can then tailor our advertising message specifically for them.

## Portfolio management

Since its arrival on the business scene in the early 1970s, portfolio management has been shown to be one of the most powerful strategic planning tools to emerge this century. However, a word of caution is advisable. First, their prescriptions should not be applied blindly; second, the particular version used is less important than the analytical depth and creativity with which it is applied. What this means will become clear later.

Portfolio planning can be defined as the use of graphic models to develop a relationship between two (or more) variables judged by the manager to be of significance in a given strategic planning context.

## Product portfolio

We might well imagine that at any point in time a review of a company's different products would reveal different stages of growth, maturity and decline. In Figure 6.9 the dotted line represents the time of our analysis, and this shows one product in

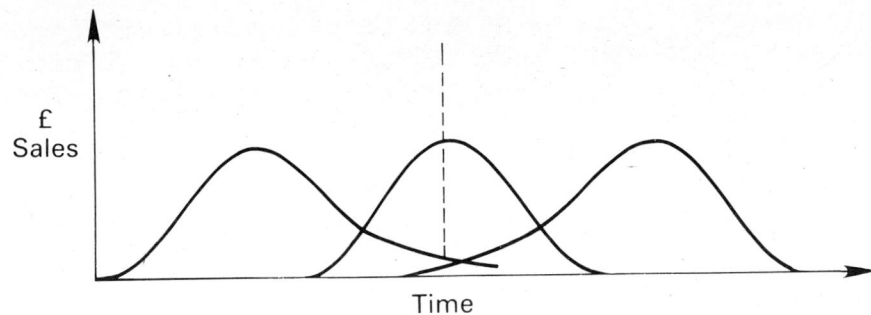

**Figure 6.9　A no-growth portfolio**

severe decline, one product in its introductory stage and one in the saturation stage.

If our objective is to grow in profitability over a long period of time, our analysis of our product portfolio should reveal a situation like the one in Figure 6.10, in which new product introductions are timed so as to ensure continuous sales growth.

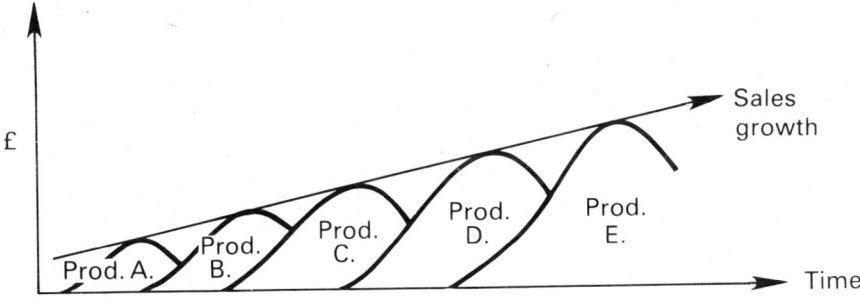

**Figure 6.10　A growth portfolio**

The idea of a portfolio is for a company to meet its objectives by balancing sales growth, cash flow and risk. As individual products progress or decline, and as markets grow or shrink, then the overall nature of the company's product portfolio will change. It is therefore essential that the whole portfolio is reviewed regularly and that an active policy towards new product development and divestment of old products is pursued. In this respect, the work of the Boston Consulting Group over the past decade has had a profound effect on the way managements think about this subject and about their product/market strategy.

## The Boston matrix

The so-called Boston matrix involves two dimensions. One is concerned with *market share*, the other with *market growth*.

It is a well-known fact that we become better at doing things the more we do them. This phenomenon is known as the 'learning curve'. It manifests itself especially with items such as labour efficiency, work specialization and methods improvement. Such benefits are themselves a part of what we call the 'experience effect', which includes such items as process innovations, better productivity from plant and equipment, product design improvements, and so on. In addition to the experience effect, and not necessarily mutually exclusive, are 'economies of scale' that come with growth. For example, capital costs do not increase in direct proportion to capacity, which results in lower overhead charges per unit of output, lower operating costs in the form of the number of operatives, lower marketing, sales, administration, and research and development costs, and lower raw materials and shipping costs.

There is an overwhelming body of evidence to show that this is so, thus it follows that the greater your volume, the lower your unit costs should be. Thus, irrespective of what happens to the price of your product, providing you have the highest market share (hence the biggest volume), you should be relatively more profitable than your competitors.

Thus, as a general rule, it can be said that market share *per se* is a desirable goal. However, we have to be certain that we have carefully defined our market, or segment. This explains why it is apparently possible for many small firms to be profitable in large markets. The reason is, of course, that in reality they have a large share of a smaller market segment. This is another reason why understanding market segmentation is the key to successful marketing. It would be unusual if there were not exceptions to the above 'law'; nevertheless, it should be noted that the evidence provided by the Boston Consulting Group shows overwhelmingly that in general these 'laws' apply universally, whether for consumer, industrial or service markets.

The importance of the *market growth* dimension in this analysis is simply that if we wish to maintain the cost advantage that a high relative market share brings, then we must grow at least as fast as the market is growing. In growth markets this has clear implications for cash usage; that is, the faster our growth rate, the higher the demands for working capital.

In markets which are going through a period of high growth, it is fairly obvious that the most sensible policy to pursue would be to gain market share by taking a bigger proportion of the market growth than your competitors. However, such a policy is very costly in promotional terms. So many companies prefer to sit tight and enjoy rates of growth lower than the market rate. The major problem with this approach is that they are in fact losing market share, which gives cost advantages (hence margin advantages) to competitors.

Since we know from previous experience of product life-cycles that the market growth rate will fall, when this stage is reached and the market inevitably becomes price sensitive and our costs are high relative to the competition, the product will begin to lose money and we will probably be forced out of the market. Indeed, seen in this light, it becomes easier to understand the reasons for the demise of many British industries, such as the motorcycle industry (discussed in more detail in Ch. 1), in which the output of the Japanese increased from thousands of units to millions of units during a period of market growth, while the output of the British remained steady during the same period. When the market growth rate started to decline, the inevitable happened. Even worse, it is virtually impossible to recover from such a situation, while the Japanese, with their advantageous cost position, have now dominated practically every market segment including big bikes.

The Boston Consulting Group combined these ideas in the form of a simple matrix, which has profound implications for the firm, especially in respect of cash flow. Profits are not always an appropriate indicator of portfolio performance. Cash flow, on the other hand, is a key determinant of a company's ability to develop its product portfolio.

The Boston matrix classifies a firm's products according to their cash usage and their cash generation along the two-dimensions described above – that is, relative market share and market growth rate. Market share is used because it is an indicator of the product's ability to generate cash; market growth is used because it is an indicator of the product's cash requirements. The measure of market share used is the product's share *relative* to the firm's largest competitor. This is important because it reflects the degree of dominance enjoyed by the product in the market. For example, if Company A has 20 per cent market share and its biggest competitor also has 20 per cent market share, this position is usually less favourable than if Company A had 20 per cent market share and its biggest competitor had only 10 per cent market share. The relative ratios would be 1 : 1 compared with 2 : 1. It is this ratio, or measure of market dominance, that the horizontal axis measures. This is summarized in Figure 6.11.

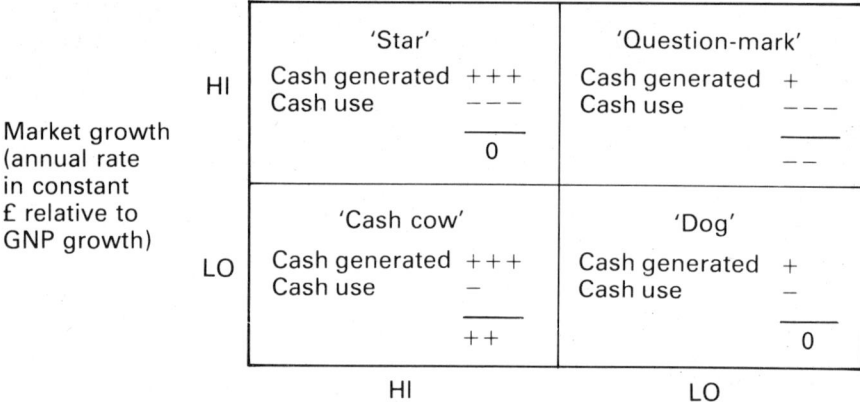

Market growth
(annual rate
in constant
£ relative to
GNP growth)

Relative market share
(ratio of company share to share of largest
competitor)

**Figure 6.11   The Boston matrix**

The definition of high relative market share is often taken to be a ratio of 1·5 : 1 or more. The cut-off point for high as opposed to low market growth should be defined according to the prevailing circumstances in the industry and the economy.

The somewhat picturesque labels attached to each of the four categories of products give some indication of the prospects for products in each quadrant. Thus the 'question-mark' is a product which has not yet achieved a dominant market position but has slipped back. It will be a high user of cash because it is in a growth market. This is also sometimes referred to as a 'wildcat'. The 'star' is probably a newish product that has achieved a high market share and thus is probably more or less self-financing in cash terms. The 'cash cows' are leaders in markets where there is little additional growth, but a lot of stability. These are excellent generators of cash and tend to use little because of the state of the market. 'Dogs' have little future and are often a cash drain on the company. They are probably candidates for divestment, although often such products fall into a category aptly described by Peter Drucker as 'investments in managerial ego'.

The art of product portfolio management now becomes a lot clearer. What we should be seeking to do is to use the surplus cash generated by the 'cash cows' to invest in our 'stars' and to invest in a selected number of 'question-marks'. This is indicated in Figure 6.12.

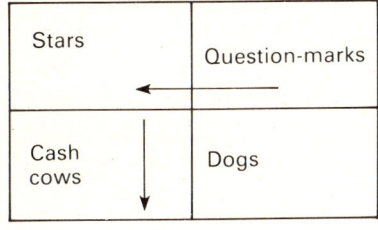

(a) Ideal product development sequence

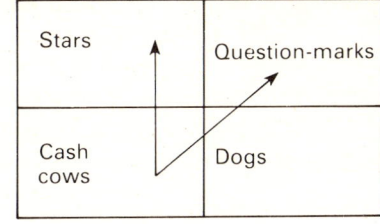

(b) Internal flow of funds

**Figure 6.12    Product development and the flow of funds**

The Boston matrix can be used to forecast the market position of our products, say, five years from now if we continue to pursue our current policies. Figure 6.13 illustrates this process for a manufacturer of plastic valves. The area of each circle is proportional to each product's contribution to total company sales volume. In the case of this particular company, it can be seen that they are following what could well prove to be disastrous policies in respect of their principal products.

Such a framework also easily helps to explain the impracticability of marketing objectives such as 'to achieve a 10 per cent growth and a 20 per cent return on investment' on each product. Such an objective, while fine as an *overall* policy if applied to individual products in the portfolio, clearly becomes a nonsense and totally self-defeating. For example, to accept a 10 per cent growth rate in a market which is growing at, say, 15 per cent per annum, is likely to prove disastrous in the long run. Likewise, to go for a much higher than market growth rate in a low-growth market is certain to lead to unnecessary price wars and market disruption.

This type of framework is particularly useful for demonstrating to senior management the implications of different product/market

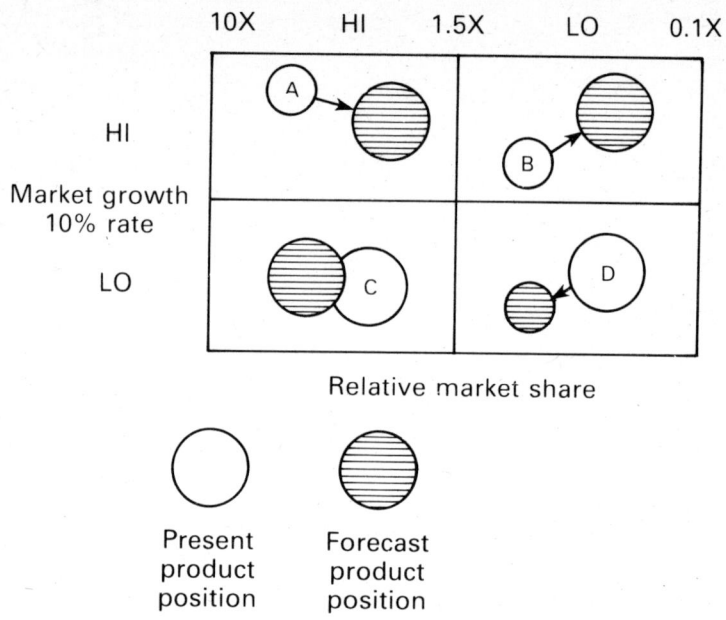

Figure 6.13   **The product portfolio, current and projected**

strategies. It is also useful in formulating policies towards new product development.

## The directional policy matrix

Another useful tool in developing a viable, long-term product portfolio is the directional policy matrix, which was independently developed by Shell and General Electric. Whilst there are some similarities with the Boston matrix, there are some important differences. The directional policy matrix uses *industry attractiveness* and *business strengths* as the two main axes, and bases these dimensions upon a number of variables. Using these variables, and some scheme for weighting them according to their importance, products (or businesses) are classified into one of nine cells in a 3-×-3 matrix. Thus the same purpose is served as in the Boston matrix (i.e. comparing investment opportunities among products or businesses) but with the difference that multiple criteria are used. These criteria vary according to circumstances, but generally include those shown in Figure 6.14.

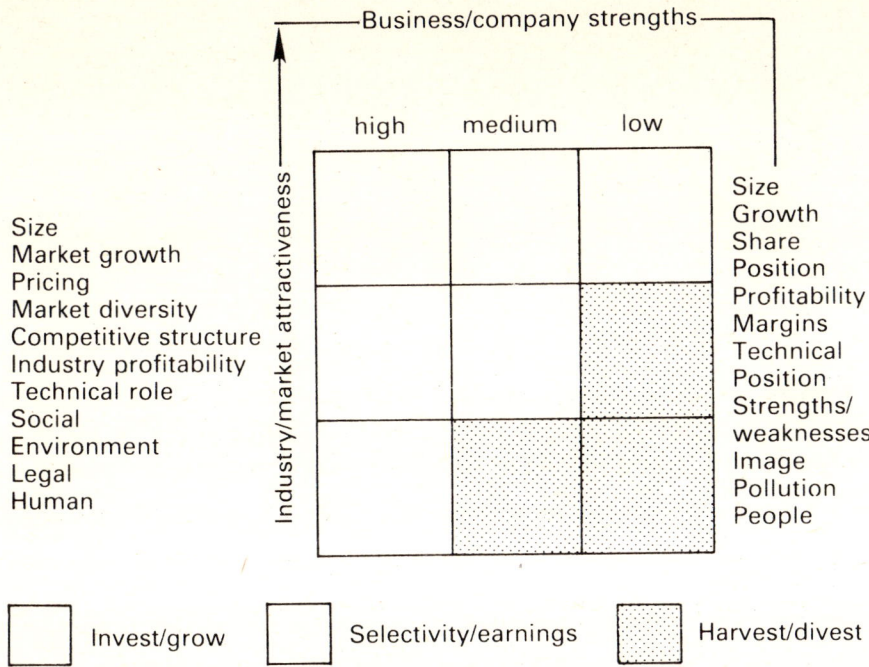

**Figure 6.14   The directional policy matrix**

The criteria listed in Figure 6.14 are expanded in Table 6.2. It will be seen that this list is totally consistent with the concept of the marketing audit. A rating and weighting system can then be applied to potential opportunities to assess their suitability or otherwise. A worked example is provided in Figure 6.15.

Whatever portfolio model is used, it can be seen that obvious consideration should be given towards marketing objectives and strategies which are appropriate to the attractiveness of a market and the extent to which such opportunities match our capabilities. The general guidelines which are given in Figure 6.16 can be applied to both the Boston matrix and the directional policy matrix.

One final word of warning is necessary. Such general guidelines should not be followed unquestioningly. They are intended more as checklists of questions that should be asked about each major product in each major market *before* setting marketing objectives and strategies.

**Table 6.2**
**Factors contributing to market attractiveness and business position**

| Attractiveness of your market | Status/position of your business |
| --- | --- |
| Market factors | Your share (in equivalent |
| Size (money units or both) | terms) |
| Size of key segments | Your share of key segments |
| Growth rate per year: | Your annual growth rate: |
| total | total |
| segments | segments |
| Diversity of market | Diversity of your participation |
| Sensitivity to price, service | Your influence on the market |
| features and external | |
| factors | Lags or leads in your sales |
| Cyclicality | |
| Seasonality | Bargaining power of your |
| Bargaining power of | suppliers |
| upstream suppliers | Bargaining power of your |
| Bargaining power of | customers |
| downstream suppliers | |
| | Where you fit, how you |
| Competition | compare in terms of |
| Types of competitors | products, marketing |
| Degree of concentration | capability, service, |
| Changes in type and mix | production strength, |
| | financial strength, |
| Entries and exits | management |
| Changes in share | |
| Substitution by new | Segments you have entered |
| technology | or left |
| Degrees and types of | Your relative share change |
| integration | Your vulnerability to new |
| | technology |
| Financial and economic | Your own level of integration |
| factors | |
| Contribution margins | Your margins |
| Leveraging factors, such as | Your scale and experience |
| economics of scale and | |
| experience | |

**Table 6.2** (*continued*)

| Attractiveness of your market | Status/position of your business |
| --- | --- |
| Barriers to entry or exit (both financial and non-financial) | Barriers to your entry or exit (both financial and non-financial) |
| Capacity utilization | Your capacity utilization |
| Technological factors | Your ability to cope with change |
| Maturity and volatility | |
| Complexity | Depths of your skills |
| Differentiation | Types of your technological skills |
| Patents and copyrights | |
| Manufacturing process technology required | Your patent protection |
| | Your manufacturing technology |
| Sociopolitical factors in your environment | |
| Social attitudes and trends | Your company's responsiveness and flexibility |
| Laws and government agency regulations | Your company's ability to cope |
| Influence with pressure groups and government representatives | Your company's aggressiveness |
| Human factors, such as unionization and community acceptance | Your company's relationships |

Finally, in this discussion of portfolio management it is important to recognize the strategic connection between the life-cycle and relative market share and market growth. Figure 6.17 illustrates the consequences of failing to appreciate the implications of both the product life-cycle concept and the dual combination of market share and market growth.

Companies A and B both start out with question-marks (wildcats) in years 5 and 6 in a growing market. Company A invests in building market share and quickly turns the product into a star. Company B,

| Factor | Scoring Criteria | | | Score | Weighting | Ranking |
|--------|:---:|:---:|:---:|:---:|:---:|:---:|
| | *10* | *5* | *0* | | | |
| 1 Market size (£ Millions) | ⩾£250 | £51.250 | ⩽£50 | 5 | 15 | 0.75 |
| 2 Volume growth (Units) | ⩾10% | 5.9% | <5% | 10 | 25 | 2.5 |
| 3 Competitive Intensity | Low | Medium | High | 6 | 10 | 0.6 |
| 4 Industry Profitability | >15% | 10.15% | <10% | 8 | 25 | 2.0 |
| 5 Vulnerability | Low | Medium | High | 6 | 15 | 0.9 |
| 6 Cyclicality | Low | Medium | High | 2.5 | 10 | 0.25 |

TOTAL = 7.0

*Note:* This form illustrates a quantitative approach to evaluating market attractiveness. Each factor is score multiplied by the percentage weighting and totalled for the overall score. In this example, an overall score of 7 out of 10 places this market in the highly attractive category.

**Figure 6.15   Scoring market attractiveness**

meanwhile, manages its product for profit over a four-year period so that, while still growing, it steadily loses market share (i.e. it remains a question-mark or wildcat).

In year 10, when the market becomes saturated (when typically competitive pressures intensify), Company B, with its low market share (hence typically higher costs and lower margins), cannot compete and quickly drops out of the market. Company A, on the other hand, aggressively defends its market share and goes on to enjoy a period of approximately tens years with a product which has become a cash cow. Thus Company B, by pursuing a policy of short-term profit maximization, lost at least ten years' profit potential.

It will be recalled that earlier the need was identified to complete a full and detailed marketing audit prior to setting marketing objectives. Such analyses as those described in this chapter should be an integral part of that marketing audit; life-cycles and portfolio matrices can provide key indicators of present and future market positions.

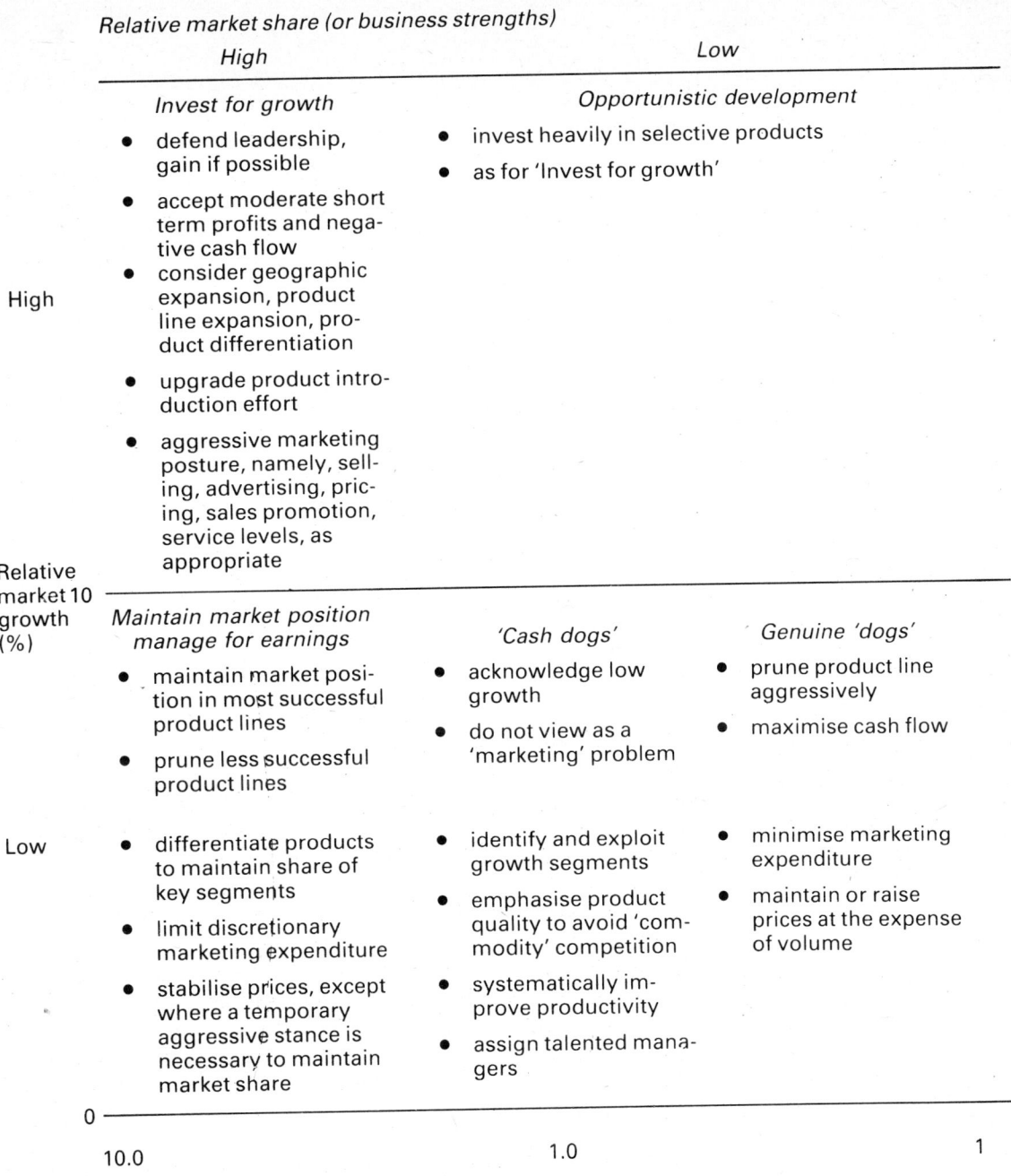

Figure 6.16 **Strategies suggested by portfolio matrix analysis**

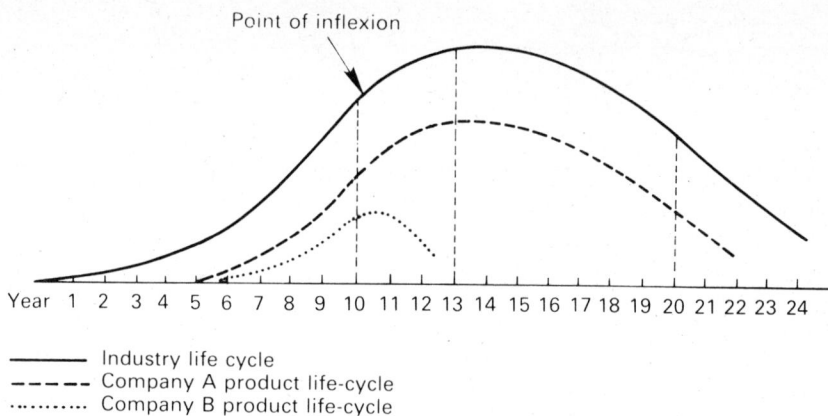

Figure 6.17   **Short-term profit maximization versus market share and long-term profit maximization**

The marketing audit should contain a product life-cycle for each major brand and product sub-class and an attempt should be made (using the audit information) to predict the future shape of the life-cycle. It should also contain a product portfolio matrix showing the present position of the products and the future desired position of the same products (e.g. for five years ahead, if this is the planning horizon). The matrix may therefore have to include some products not currently in the range.

# Overview

Before explaining how to conduct strategic analysis and corporate planning, the relationship between strategic marketing planning and corporate planning must be understood.

Corporate planning involves five steps: setting the long-term financial objectives; conducting a management audit; setting objectives and strategies; producing detailed one-year plans and, finally, incorporating these plans into the greater corporate plan. Such a plan provides a company with a better base for long-term stability than those plans which result from intuition or extrapolation.

The differences between a corporate objective and a marketing objective are described, as well as the importance of consistency with the total strategic plan. The overall corporate objective is long-term profitability, with corporate strategies, including market-ing objectives, being the means of achieving the main corporate objective.

Marketing objectives can be seen within the light of the Ansoff matrix, which describes four main categories of objectives. Once objectives have been set, companies will need to fill the gap between objectives and forecasts.

Understanding the nature of products, and in particular the product life-cycle, is central to achieving objectives. However, if companies are not going to fall into the trap of total product-orientation, they must view products and their life-cycle within the context of market behaviour and development. The concept of diffusion of innovation helps us plot the likely acceptance of a new product and to some extent manage its introduction and deployment in the market-place.

The chapter concludes with a detailed look at portfolio management, a powerful strategic planning tool if used with discrimination. By using graphic models to show a relationship between two or more important variables, a portfolio can be planned in the strategic planning process. Two tools, the Boston matrix and the directional policy matrix are discussed.

Both the life-cycle and the portfolio analyses are useful indicators of current and future market positions, and therefore integral to the marketing audit which helps companies set marketing objectives.

# Part II
# EXECUTIVE ACTION

# Action guide 1
# Reviewing current practice

This 'action guide' is designed to enable you to take a 'helicopter view' of the way your company does its planning and then to home in on the areas where improvements can be made. Moreover, this material will enable you to identify information gaps that might be unknown to you at present.

# MARKETING PLANNING PROCESS QUESTIONNAIRE

*Note:* Although care has been taken to use generally accepted terminology in the wording of this questionnaire, there will always be the company that uses different words. For example, when we talk about return on investment (ROI), other companies might well use other expressions or measures, such as return on capital employed, value added, and so on.

1 With this caveat in mind, will you please turn to the questionnaire and respond to it by putting a tick against each question in one of the four columns provided.

2 After completing the questionnaire, add up how many ticks you listed under 'not applicable'. It is our experience that if you have more than eight ticks, then you could be refusing to acknowledge some aspects of planning that are generally covered by most companies. Reappraise your scoring on these if required.

# Questionnaire

| *Corporate issues* | Yes | No | Don't know | Not applic. |
|---|---|---|---|---|
| • Is there a corporate statement about | | | | |
|    – the nature of the company's current business mission? | | | | |
|    – its vision of the future? | | | | |
| • Is there a target figure for ROI? | | | | |
| • Is there a corporate plan to channel the company resources to this end? | | | | |
| • Are there defined business boundaries in terms of | | | | |
|    – products or services (that will be offered)? | | | | |
|    – customers or markets (to deal with)? | | | | |
|    – production facilities? | | | | |
|    – distribution facilities? | | | | |
|    – size and character of the workforce? | | | | |
|    – sources and levels of funding? | | | | |
| • Are there objectives for promoting the corporate image with | | | | |
|    – the stock market? | | | | |
|    – customers? | | | | |
|    – the local community? | | | | |
|    – the employees? | | | | |
|    – environmentalist/conservationist lobby? | | | | |
|    – government departments? | | | | |
|    – trade associations, etc.? | | | | |

## Marketing issues

|  | Yes | No | Don't know | Not applic. |
|---|---|---|---|---|

- Is there a marketing plan?
- Is it compatible with the corporate plan?
- Does it cover the same period?
- Is the marketing plan regularly reviewed?
- Is the plan based on an assessment of market potential or past performance?
- Will the plan close the 'gap' if carried out?
- Is there a marketing plan by product/service?
- Do relevant managers have a copy of the marketing plan?
- Are the following factors monitored in a regular and conscious way, in terms of how they affect the company's business prospects?

*Business environment:*

- economic factors?
- political/legal factors?
- fiscal factors?
- technological developments?
- intra-company issues?

*The market:*

- Trends in market size/growth in volume? in value?

- Developments/trends in product use?
  product demand?
  product presentation?
  accessories?
  substitutes?

- Developments/trends in prices?
  terms and conditions?
  trade practices?

| | Yes | No | Don't know | Not applic. |
|---|---|---|---|---|
| – Developments/trends in physical distribution? | | | | |
|     channels of distribution? | | | | |
|     purchasing patterns? | | | | |
|     stockholding? | | | | |
|     turnover? | | | | |
| – Developments/trends in communications? | | | | |
|     use of sales force? | | | | |
|     advertising? | | | | |
|     promotions? | | | | |
|     exhibitions? | | | | |
| *Competition:* | | | | |
| – Developments/trends of competitors? | | | | |
|     their marketing strategies? | | | | |
|     their strengths? | | | | |
|     new entrants? | | | | |
|     mergers/acquisitions? | | | | |
|     their reputation? | | | | |
| *The industry:* | | | | |
| – activities of trade association(s)? | | | | |
| – interfirm comparisons? | | | | |
| – industry profitability? | | | | |
| – investment levels of competitors? | | | | |
| – changes in cost structure? | | | | |
| – investment prospects? | | | | |
| – technological developments? | | | | |
| – sources of raw materials? | | | | |
| – energy utilization? | | | | |

## SWOT analysis

|  | Yes | No | Don't know | Not applic. |
|---|---|---|---|---|

- Is there someone (individual or group) responsible for converting the analysis of factors in the previous section (Marketing issues) into a summary which highlights:
    - the company's principal strengths?
    - the company's principal weaknesses (in terms of relating to external opportunities/threats)?
- Does this person(s) have access to the necessary information?
- Is this person(s) sufficiently senior for his analysis to make impact?
- Is the organizational climate such that a full and accurate analysis is seen as a striving for improvement rather than an attack on specific departments or vested interests?

## Assumptions

- Is there a set of assumptions around which the marketing plan is formulated?
- Are there assumptions made explicit to senior company personnel?
- Do they cover:
    - the business environment?
    - the market?
    - the competitors?
    - the industry?
- Are the assumptions valid in the light of current and predicted trading situations?

## Marketing objectives/strategies

|  | Yes | No | Don't know | Not applic. |
|---|---|---|---|---|
| • Are the marketing objectives clearly stated and consistent with the corporate objectives? | | | | |
| • Are there clear strategies for achieving the stated marketing objectives? | | | | |
| • Are sufficient resources made available? | | | | |
| • Are all responsibilities and authority clearly made known? | | | | |
| • Are there agreed objectives about: | | | | |
|    – the product range? | | | | |
|    – the value of sales? | | | | |
|    – the volume of sales? | | | | |
|    – profits? | | | | |
|    – market share? | | | | |
|    – market penetration? | | | | |
|    – number of customers? | | | | |
|    – introducing new products/services? | | | | |
|    – divesting of old products/services? | | | | |
|    – organization changes to develop company strengths? reduce company weaknesses? | | | | |

## Monitoring/evaluation

|  | Yes | No | Don't know | Not applic. |
|---|---|---|---|---|
| • Is the planning system well conceived and effective? | | | | |
| • Do control mechanisms exist to ensure planned objectives are met? | | | | |
| • Do internal communications function effectively? | | | | |
| • Are there any problems between marketing and other corporate functions? | | | | |

|  | Yes | No | Don't know | Not applic. |
|---|---|---|---|---|
| • Are people clear about their role in the planning process? | | | | |
| • Is there a procedure for dealing with non-achievement of objectives? | | | | |
| • Is there evidence that this reduces the chance of subsequent failure? | | | | |
| • Are there still unexploited opportunities? | | | | |
| • Are there still organizational weaknesses? | | | | |
| • Are the assumptions upon which the plan was based valid? | | | | |
| • Are there contingency plans in the event of objectives not being met/conditions changing? | | | | |

# THE ERROR QUESTIONNAIRE

In the previous exercise you examined the marketing planning process in your company and assessed in what ways it might have to change. In this exercise, you will look at organizational issues that underpin your company's marketing planning activity. This will enable you to identify specific areas of weakness. To be forewarned of them now is to be forearmed when you come to consider organizing for marketing planning and designing a marketing planning system for your company.

1   Please answer all the statements made in the accompanying document and add up the total scores for EReRORo.
2   Read the rationale behind this questionnaire on page 150.
3   Consider the ERROR scores. Do you agree they accurately reflect the organizational issues? Are low score totals made unduly low by just one or two individual low scores?

You are asked to answer a series of statements about your organization and its present approach to marketing planning. Only you will be aware of the actual situation that exists in your own organization and so, in this quest for genuine data, please try to be as objective as you can as you complete this document.
   Scoring method for each statement:

| (1) | (2) | (3) | (4) | (5) |
|---|---|---|---|---|
| Score 1 if you strongly disagree with the statement | Score 2 if you tend to disagree with the statement | Score 3 if you don't know whether you agree or disagree | Score 4 if you tend to agree with the statement | Score 5 if you strongly agree with the statement |

Please enter your score in the position indicated on each line.

## Questionnaire

|  | E | Re | R | O | Ro |
|---|---|---|---|---|---|
| The chief executive/directors show an active interest in marketing planning. |  |  |  |  | — |
| The chief executive/directors demonstrate their understanding of marketing planning. | — |  |  |  |  |
| The chief executive/directors use the marketing plan as a basis for making key marketing decisions. |  |  |  | — |  |
| The chief executive/directors value the people who make the planning system work. |  |  | — |  |  |
| The need for a marketing plan is explained to all managers. | — |  |  |  |  |
| There is adequate information/data upon which to base the marketing plan. |  |  | — |  |  |
| Line managers are trained to understand how the marketing planning process operates. | — |  |  |  |  |
| People are clear about their role in the marketing planning process. |  |  |  |  | — |
| Line/operational management are satisfied with the marketing plan. |  |  |  | — |  |
| Our plans tend to have a good balance between short-term and long-term objectives. |  |  | — |  |  |
| Adequate resources are allocated to the marketing planning process. |  |  | — |  |  |
| Enough time is allowed for the planning process. |  |  | — |  |  |
| It is made easy for line management to understand the marketing plan. | — |  |  |  |  |
| It is reasonable to expect a company of our size to have a well-formulated marketing plan. |  |  | — |  |  |
| Reasons for past successes or failures are analysed. |  |  | — |  |  |
| In our organization we don't leave planning just to the planners. |  |  |  |  | — |
| Our organizational structure is conducive to a sound planning process. |  |  | — |  |  |

|  | E | Re | R | O | Ro |
|---|---|---|---|---|---|
| There is a clear understanding of the marketing terminology as it is used in the company. | — | | | | |
| Market opportunities are highlighted in the company plans. | | — | | | |
| Functional specialists contribute to the marketing planning process. | | | | | — |
| We limit our activities so that we are not faced with trying to do too many things at one time. | | | — | | |
| Our organization structure is conducive to the plan being implemented. | | | | — | |
| Marketing jargon is kept to a minimum. | | | | — | |
| Only essential data appears in our plans. | | | — | | |
| From the wealth of data available to us, we are successful in picking out key issues. | — | | | | |
| There is a balance between narrative explanation and numerical data in our plans. | | | — | | |
| Our field sales force operates in a way that is supportive to our marketing plan. | | | | | — |
| Our plans demonstrate a high level of awareness of the macro issues facing us. | — | | | | |
| People make a diligent attempt to provide accurate inputs to the planning process. | | — | | | |
| Marketing planning in our organization is a serious and meaningful activity. | | | — | | |
| Our plan takes into account the major problems and opportunities faced by the organization. | | | | — | |
| There is a high level of awareness of the micro issues in our plans. | — | | | | |
| Our plans recognize that ways for developing business (long term) have to be matched against short-term operations. | | — | | | |
| Inputs to the marketing planning process are an integral part of the job of all line managers. | | | | | — |

| | E | Re | R | O | Ro |
|---|---|---|---|---|---|
| Marketing planning rates as a priority issue in our organization. | | | | — | |
| Our planning inputs are not 'massaged' to satisfy the directors of the company. | | | — | | |
| Overall, people believe our planning system is not too bureaucratic. | — | | | | |
| We use the same time scale for our marketing plans as we do for distribution, production, finance and personnel plans. | | | — | | |
| We view the operational plan as the first year of our long-term plan, not as a separate entity. | | | | — | |
| The chief executive/directors do not see themselves as operating beyond the confines of the marketing plan. | | | | | — |
| The advocates of 'correct' marketing planning are senior enough in the company to influence policy/decisions. | | | | | — |
| People are always given clear instructions about the nature of their expected contribution to the marketing plan. | | | — | | |
| Pro-forma sheets are provided to make data collection easy. | | | — | | |
| Our marketing plans do not go into too much detail. | | | — | | |
| The role of specialists is made quite clear in our planning process. | | | | | — |

Add up your score in each column (max. 45).

## The rationale behind the ERROR questionnaire

There are many ways of looking at organizations and establishing 'models' of how they operate. One very common model is the organization chart, which attempts to show how responsibility is distributed throughout the company and to clarify the chains of command.

Other models are derived from the inputs and outputs of the company. For example, a financial model is built up by analysing all the necessary financial inputs required to conduct the business and monitoring the efficiency by which these are converted into sales revenue.

The ERROR questionnaire is based on a particularly useful model, one which helps us to understand the relationship between different facets of the organization. By understanding the nature of these relationships, we are better placed to introduce organizational change – in this case, an improved marketing planning system.

There are three main assumptions behind this model.

- That the organization today is to some extent (often very strongly) conditioned by its historical background. For example, if historically there has never been a pressing need for a comprehensive marketing planning system because of favourable trading conditions, then this will be reflected in the current planning system and the attitudes of the company's staff.

- That the organization today is to some extent (sometimes strongly) conditioned and directed by its future goals. For example, the company that senses its marketing planning processes need to improve will take steps to introduce changes. That these changes will make impact on organizational life is self-evident. Furthermore, much of the resistance to be overcome will stem from the 'historical' forces mentioned above.

- What actually happens in an organization is determined by the skills, knowledge, experience and beliefs of the organization's personnel. Thus at the heart of any organization is the collective expertise or 'education' at its disposal. This will ultimately determine the success it has in any work it undertakes, whether it is making goods or providing services.

Clearly, then, the level of so-called *education* will also be a determining factor in the quality and scope of the company's marketing planning process.

These assumptions provide the 'skeleton' of our organizational model. This is shown in Figure AG1.1. There are still important elements missing from this model. Irrespective of the company's corporate sum of available skills and knowledge, nothing can be produced without physical *resources* being made available.

The key resources required for marketing planning will be accurate data, means of storing and retrieving the data, adequate

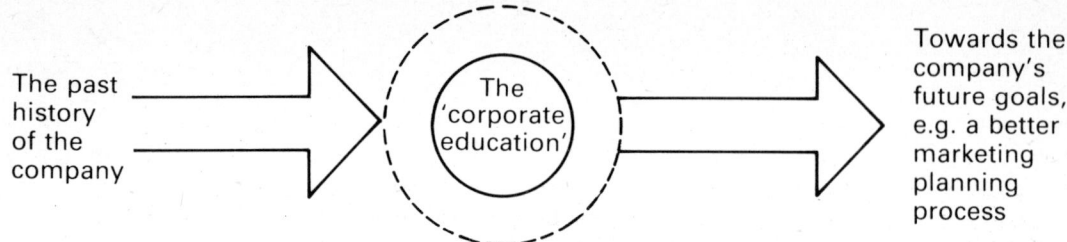

The past history of the company

The 'corporate education'

Towards the company's future goals, e.g. a better marketing planning process

**Figure A G1.1    Skeleton organizational model**

staff and time to analyse the data. But having the right resources isn't the whole solution, the company must also develop the best systems or *routines* to optimize the use of these resources. In marketing planning terms, concern is likely to focus on routines associated with collecting data, evaluating past performance, spotting marketing opportunities, sifting essential information from non-essential information, and so on.

Routines, however, do not necessarily look after themselves. As soon as any system is set up, *roles and relationships* need to be defined; who is going to do what to ensure that things happen. Again, in marketing planning terms this will call into question the role of various members of staff from the chief executive downwards. How clear are people about their role in the planning process? Should planning just be left to the planning department? What is the role of functional specialists? Who actually collects marketing data? Who do they present it to? Many questions have to be answered if the subsequent routines are going to function smoothly.

Even this isn't the end of the story, because once roles are defined there is still the problem of setting up the right *organizational structure and climate*, one that will enable people to fulfil their roles in a productive way. From a marketing planning viewpoint, structure and climate issues surface in several ways; for example, in the level of commitment to the planning process, the degree to which functional specialists are integrated into the planning process, the degree to which long-term and short-term issues are accommodated, the extent to which the company is prepared to tackle the real and important issues it faces, the openness of communications, and so on.

It is now possible to see how the completed model looks (Fig. AG1.2).

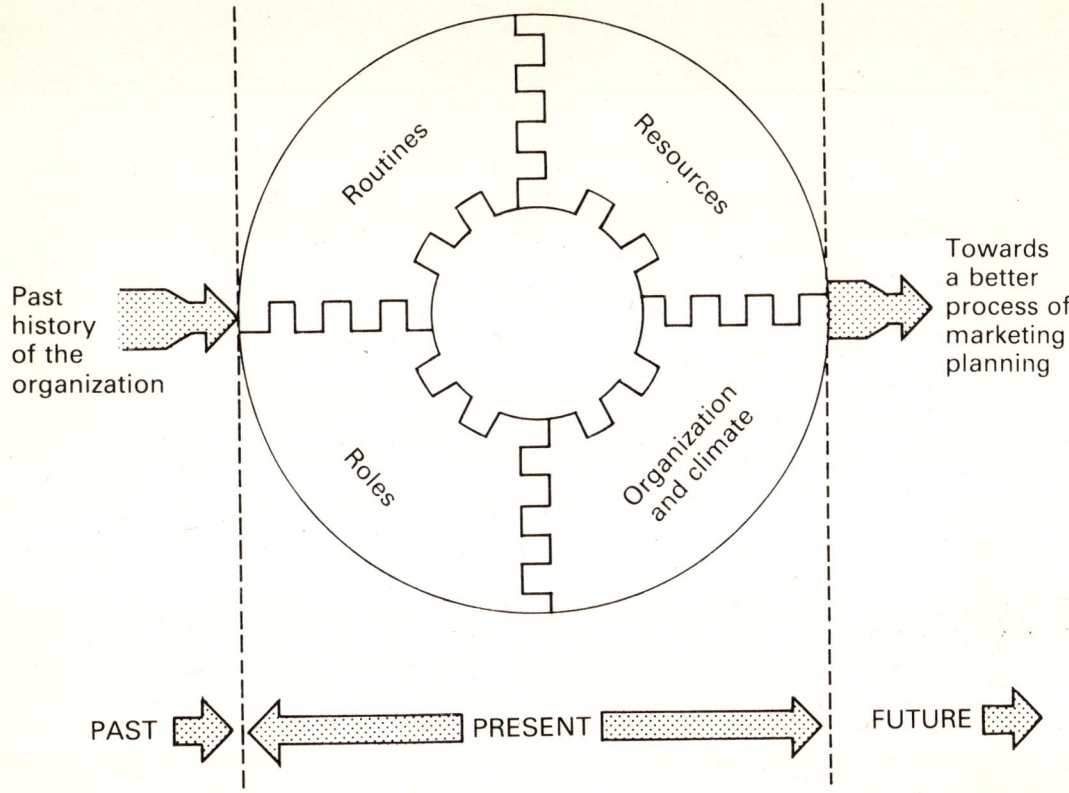

**Figure A G1.2  Completed organizational model**

From the foregoing explanation, it is possible to see how the different facets of the organization – that is,

- the 'corporate education'
- the resources
- the routines or systems
- the roles and relationships
- the organizational structure and climate

– interrelate with each other.

Thus to introduce an improved marketing planning system might involve changes in all of these areas. Some personnel might need training, more or different resources might be required, routines or systems might need improving, roles and relationships perhaps need to be reappraised and the structure and climate of the organization re-examined. Conversely, only one or two of these areas might need tackling.

The ERROR questionnaire is designed to provide a 'snapshot' of the company and to help you identify which areas might be the starting point for introducing improvements. The word ERROR is made up as follows:

| | |
|---|---|
| E | education required for company personnel |
| Re | resources available |
| R | routines (or systems) in current use |
| O | organizational structure and climate |
| Ro | roles that people play. |

These are the component parts of the model. There is a maximum score of 45 for each of these facets of the organization. For your company, the facets with the lowest scores would be those which in the first instance, merit attention.

## DESIGNING AND IMPLEMENTING A MARKETING PLANNING SYSTEM

In this final exercise, you will focus on the marketing planning system best suited to your company.

## Selecting the appropriate approach

Figure AG1.3 reproduces below a diagram from Chapter 5 which

Company size

| Market/product diversity | | Large | Medium | Small |
|---|---|---|---|---|
| | High | High formalization | High/medium formalization | Medium formalizaton |
| | Medium | High/medium formalization | Medium formalization | Low formalization |
| | Low | Medium formalization | Low formalization | Very low formalization |

**Figure A G1.3   Influences on the planning process**

shows how the degree of formalization of the marketing planning process relates to company size and the diversity of its operations.

1 Select a position on Figure AG1.3 which best describes your company's situation. This is probably the sort of marketing planning system you need to have in mind as you tackle the following section, 'Identifying the improvement areas'.
2 In the space beneath the diagram on Worksheet 1 write down a few key words or sentences that would best describe the marketing planning system you would need for your company.

## Identifying the improvement areas

1 Imagine that it is possible to measure the efficiency of a marketing planning system on scale from 0 to 100, where 100 is equivalent to a 100 per cent efficiency; that is, the system works well and conforms with your findings in the previous section. How would you rate the current approach to marketing planning in your company? To what extent does it match up with your ideal?
2 Enter your score on Worksheet 1, drawing a horizontal line as shown in Figure AG1.4. The difference between your scoreline and the ideal must represent where there is room for following the instructions given below.

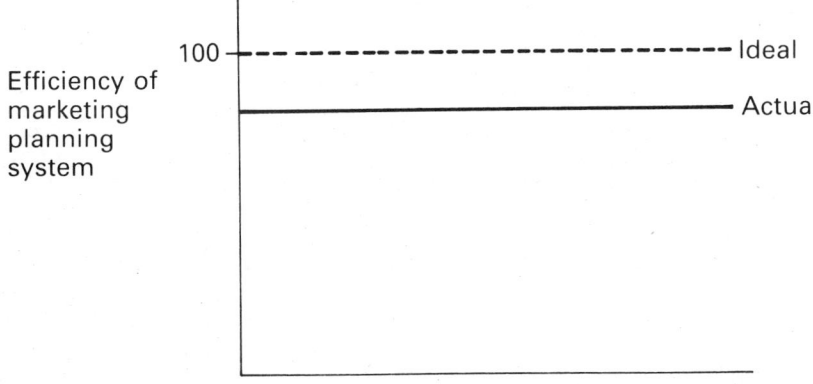

**Figure A G1.4   Force-field diagram: recording the performance score**

3  Identify all those factors that have 'pushed' your actual efficiency line below the ideal. Add them to Worksheet 1, showing them as actual forces pushing down. If you can, represent the biggest forces with longer arrows, as shown in Figure AG1.5. You will probably have more than three factors; list as many as you can. Remember you should be noting only those that affect the marketing planning system, not the company's general approach to marketing. We will call these downward forces 'restraining forces' because they are acting against improvement.

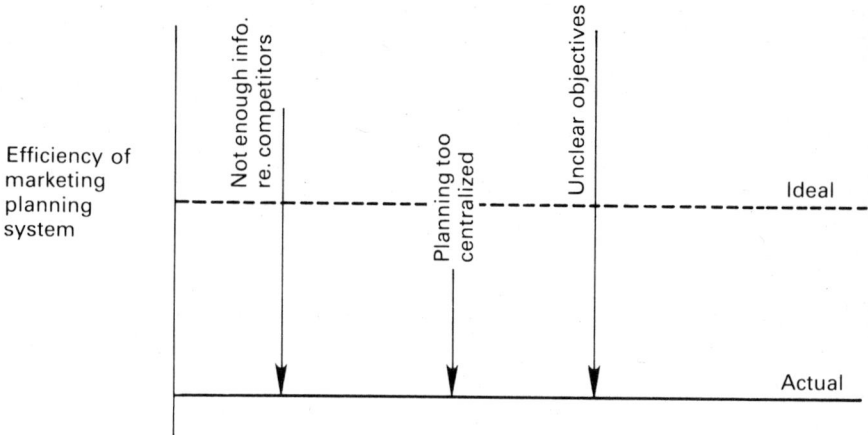

**Figure A G1.5    Force-field diagram: examples of restraining forces**

4  Now ask yourself why isn't the actual performance line you have drawn lower than it is. The reason is, of course, that there are several parts of the system that work well, or there are other strengths in your company. Identify these positive forces and add them to Worksheet 1 as shown in Figure AG1.6, again relating the arrow size approximately to the influence of each factor. Again the factors shown above are only examples. You will identify many more. We call these 'driving forces' because they are pushing towards improvement.

5  Worksheet 1 should now be complete, showing the two sets of forces lined up against each other. What next? Well, it might have struck you that what you have assembled is somewhat

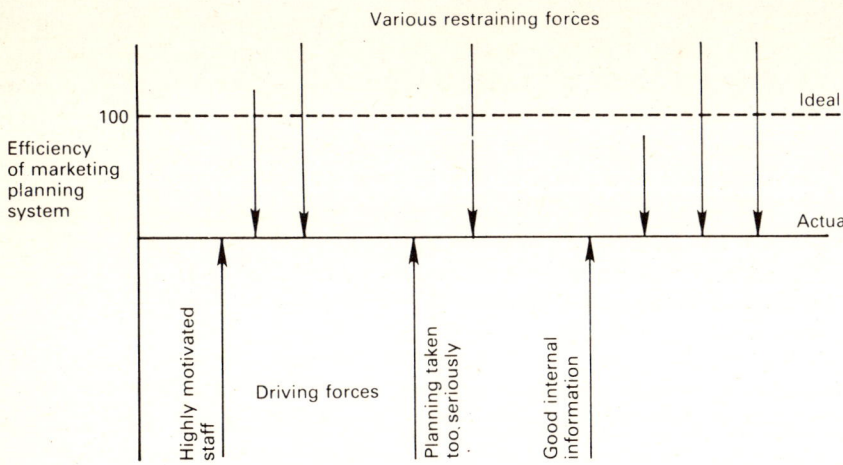

**Figure A G1.6   Force-field diagram: examples of driving forces**

analogous to a ship at sea. Your ship (the marketing planning system) is wallowing below its ideal level in the water but is prevented from sinking by buoyant forces (driving forces). To restore the ship to its correct level it would be natural to remove or jettison some of the cargo (the restraining forces), not to try and get out and push from below.

As it is for the ship, so it is for your marketing planning system, therefore:

(i)   Select the major restraining forces and work out ways that you can reduce their impact or preferably eliminate them altogether. These will be the source of the greatest improvements, but some of the remedies might need time to take effect.

(ii)   Concurrently select minor restraining forces and plan to eliminate them also. Although their impact on improvement might be less, you will probably find they respond more quickly to treatment.

(iii)   Select the smallest driving forces and work out if there are any ways to increase their impact.

*Note:* Put most of your energy into removing the restraining factors. To focus on the major driving forces – for example, trying to make highly motivated staff even more motivated – is likely to be counter-productive. Further details about force-field theory and an

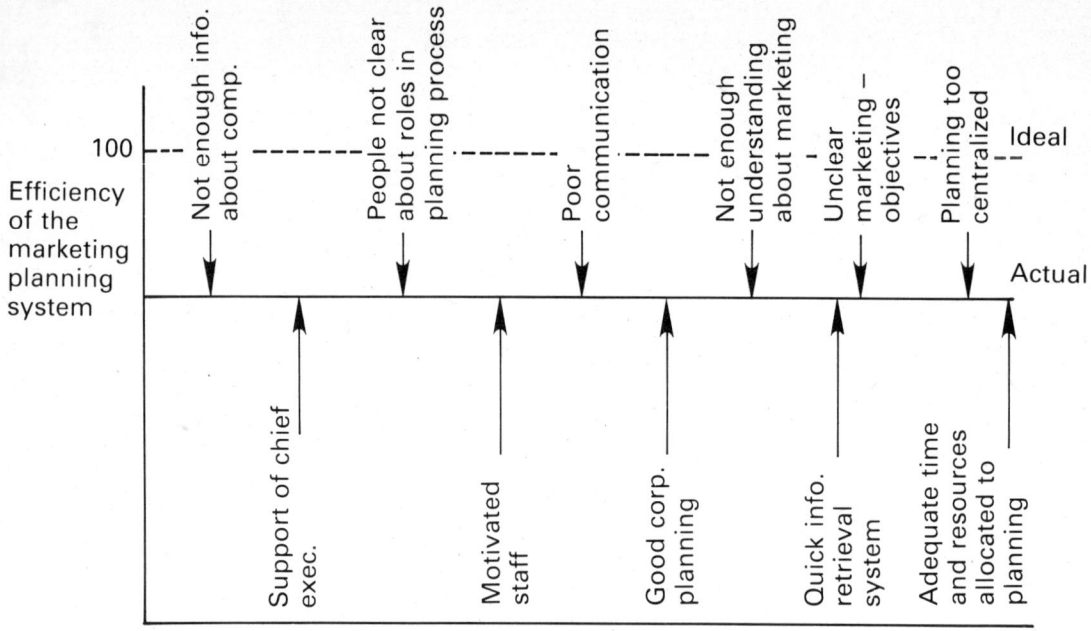

**Figure A G1.7   Example of a completed force-field diagram**

example of how Worksheet 1 might look are given in the supplementary section at the end of this book.

6   Assemble your various responses to 5 (i), (ii), and (iii) together into a comprehensive improvement plan, then take steps to get it accepted and acted upon.

7   Figure AG1.7 gives an example of how a finished force-field diagram might look, although most people will have identified several more factors than shown here. Many of the factors identified by you ought to be unique to your company.

*Note:*

● Remember that only factors that affect the marketing planning process ought to appear in the force-field diagram.
● It is possible to draw the force arrows proportional in length to their influence.

**Worksheet 1   Force-field diagram**

# Action guide 2
# Setting marketing objectives

The book goes to some lengths to explain the difference between corporate objectives and marketing objectives. It concludes that marketing objectives are solely concerned with *which products go to which markets*. It goes on to add that marketing strategies are concerned with *how* that is done.

Since marketing objectives are only concerned with products and markets an extremely useful planning aid is provided by the Ansoff matrix (Fig. AG2.1).

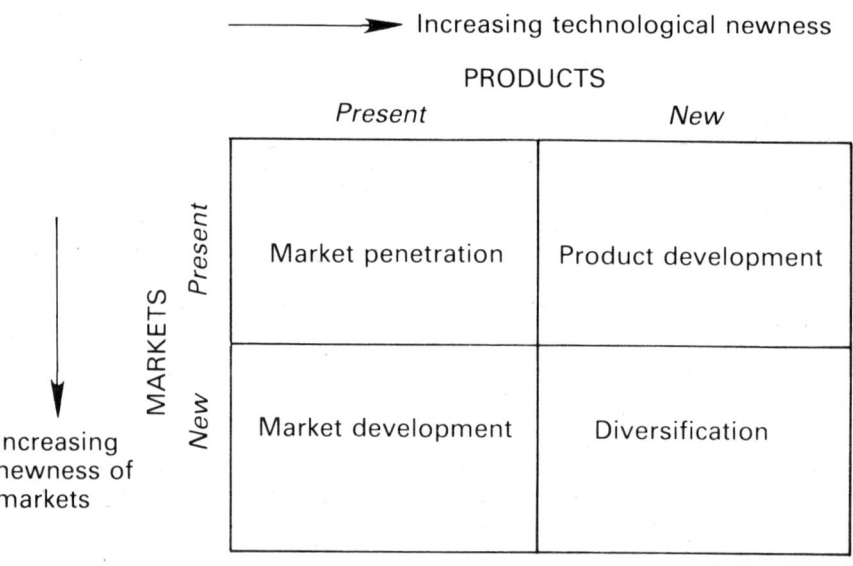

**Figure A G2.1    Ansoff matrix**

This matrix suggests there are four types of marketing objectives:

- selling established products into established markets (market penetration)
- selling established products into new markets (market extension)
- selling new products into established markets (product development)
- selling new products into new markets (diversification).

**Task 1**

Using the blank Ansoff matrix which follows (Worksheet 2), or perhaps using a larger sheet of paper, draw the matrix for your company's products and markets. Please note that when you consider whether or not a market is new or established, the question you must ask yourself is: how long does it take to get one's distinctive competence known in this market? If you have been dealing with the market for anything less than your answer to this question, then that is a new market.

Similarly, new products are those, probably, at the early stages of their life-cycles, where the company is still 'learning' how to make them; that is, it hasn't solved all the tooling, scheduling, quality, design and technical problems in the same way as it has for the established products.

**Task 2**

Combining the information on the Ansoff matrix with that of your SWOT analysis, pick out those areas of business that offer the best prospects for your company. For each one write a marketing objective for your longer-term planning horizon (i.e. 2, 3, 4, 5, 6, 7, 8, 9 or 10 years, etc). This must be quite explicit in terms of:

- product/service
- customer/market segment
- volume of sales
- market share

Now state the specific objectives for the first year of your planning horizon. The marketing objectives should be consistent with the information from the product life-cycle analysis and directional policy matrix, which follow.

**Worksheet 2   Ansoff matrix**

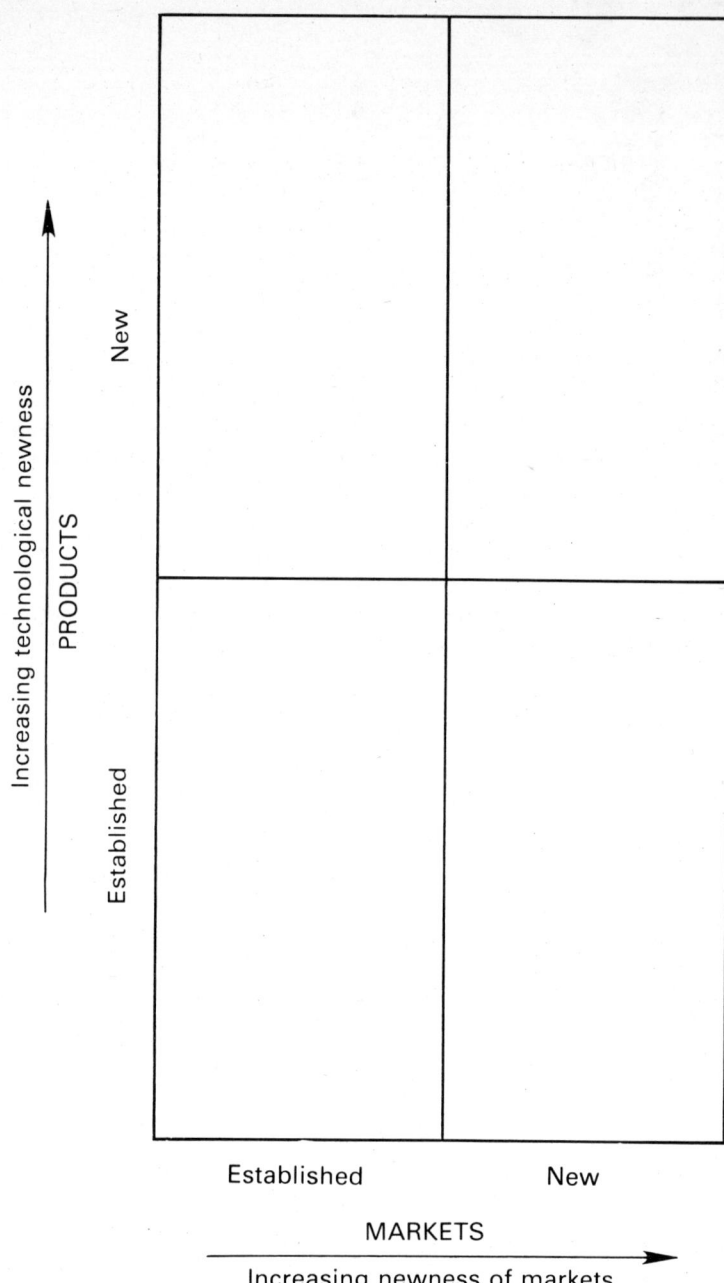

162

# Action guide 3
# Life-cycle analysis

As explained earlier, in Chapter 6, all products or services go through a life-cycle of five stages – introduction, growth, maturation, saturation and, ultimately, decline.

Depending upon the nature of the particular product and its market, the life-cycle can be of short or long duration. Similarly, different products will have different levels of sales. Nevertheless, allowing for these differences in 'width' and 'height', product life-cycle curves all have a remarkably similar and consistent shape. It is because of consistency of the life-cycle curve that this aspect of marketing management becomes such a powerful analytical tool.

The following material is designed to help you conduct a life-cycle analysis for your company's products or services. By doing this it will help to focus on information that will be used in setting marketing objectives and strategies.

1   Using Worksheet 3, invent a suitable scale for the sales volume axis; that is, one that will encompass the sales peaks you have had or are likely to experience in your business.
2   At the position marked 'current sales', record the levels of sales volume for your products or services.

*Note:* You will have to select the time scale you use. If your products are shortlived, perhaps you might have to calculate sales figures in terms of days or weeks. For longer-lived products perhaps annual sales figures will be more appropriate.

3   Taking each product in turn, plot a life-cycle curve based upon historical data at your disposal; for example, if in step 2 above you decided that a monthly sales analysis would be necessary to capture the movement on the life-cycle curves, then check back through your sales records and plot the sales volume for each product at monthly intervals.

4   From the life-cycle curves you have drawn, extend those into the future where extrapolation looks feasible – that is, where a distinct pattern exists.

*Note:* You should finish up with a worksheet looking something like the example shown in Figure AG3.1.

5   Make notes about your key findings from this exercise in the space below Worksheet 3.
6   So far you have only looked at your products in isolation. Now in the space below ( or on the same worksheet if it doesn't cause too much confusion), compare each life-cycle pattern of your major products or services with the *total market* life-cycle for each one (product sub-class).

Do your product patterns mirror the product sub-class life-cycle? Are your sales falling while the total market sales are steady or increasing? Is the reverse happening? Many outcomes will be possible, but whatever they are you are asked to explain them and to write in the space below what these comparisons between the total market and your sales tell you about your product/service range and its future prospects.

**Worksheet 3   Life-cycle analysis**

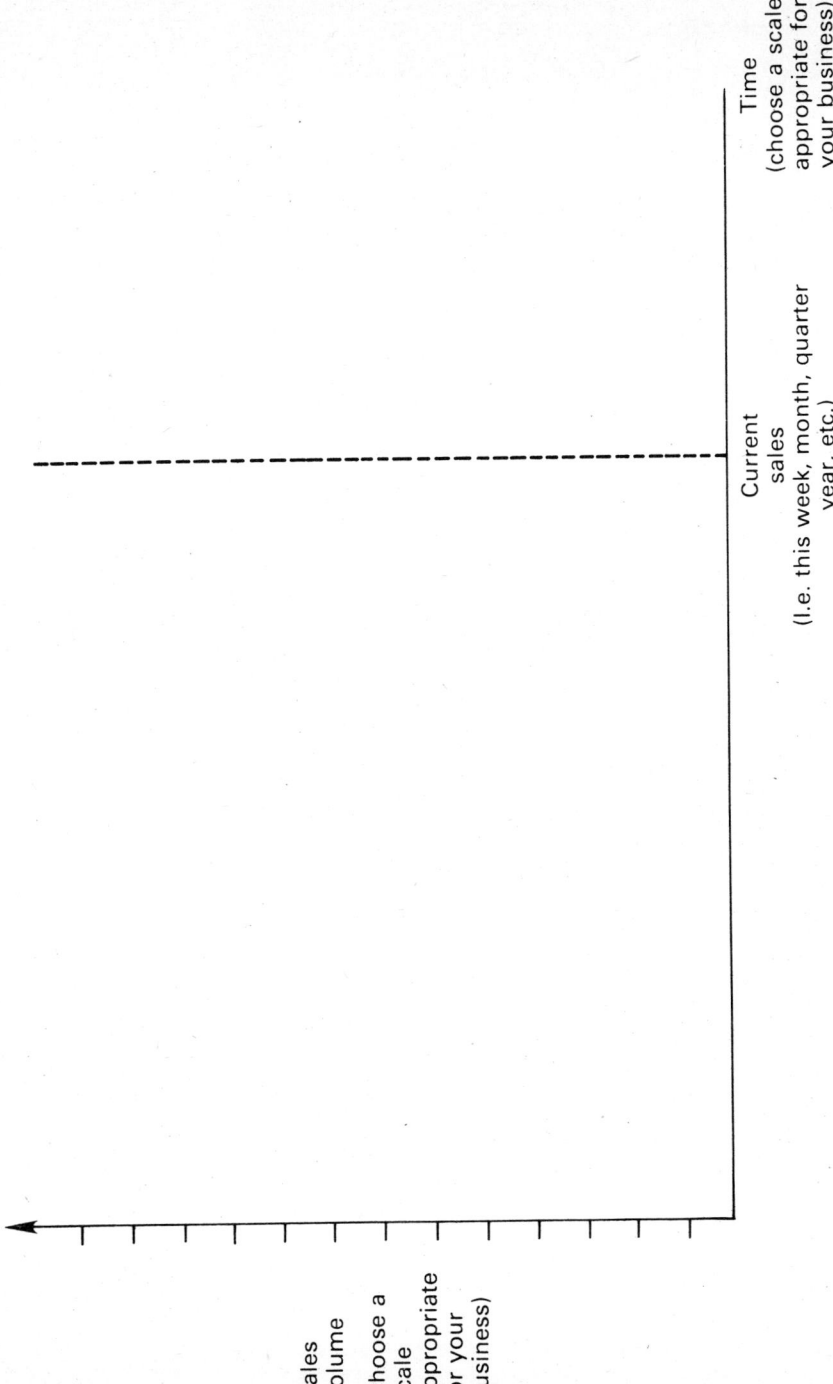

Sales
volume

(choose a
scale
appropriate
for your
business)

Current
sales
(I.e. this week, month, quarter
year, etc.)

Time
(choose a scale
appropriate for
your business)

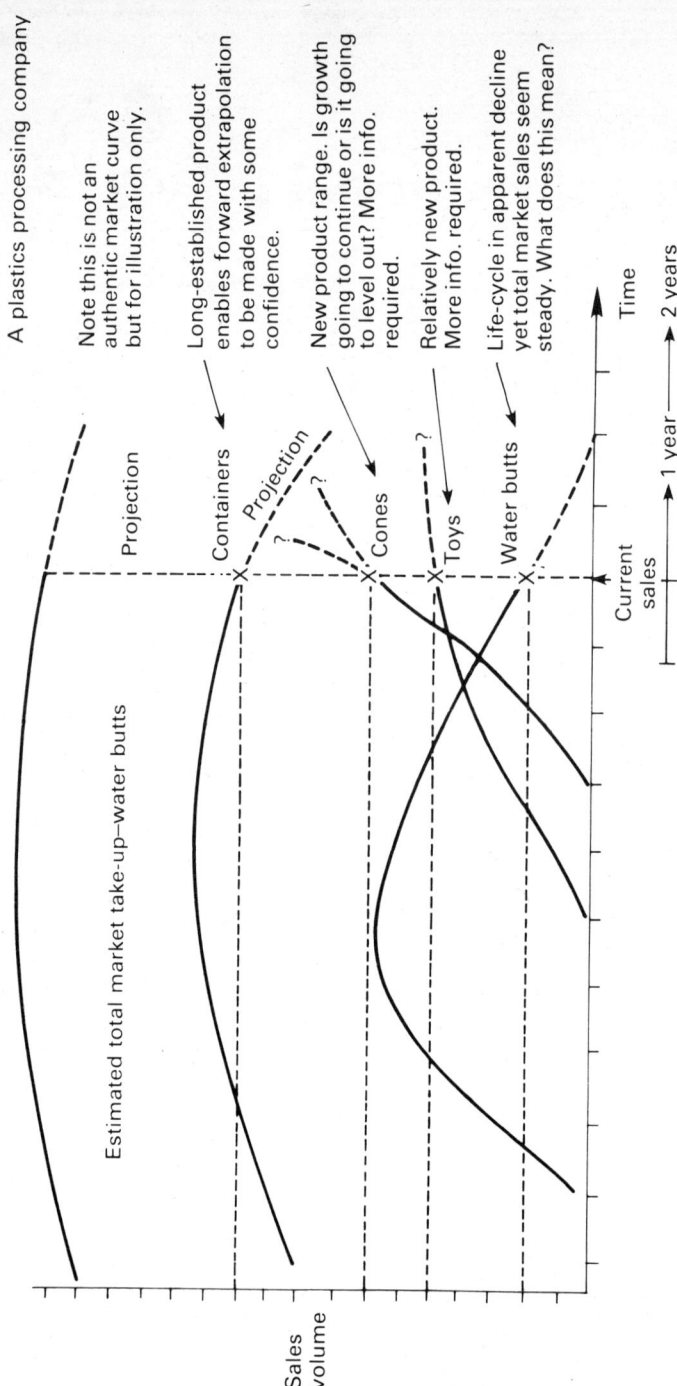

A plastics processing company

Note this is not an authentic market curve but for illustration only.

Long-established product enables forward extrapolation to be made with some confidence.

New product range. Is growth going to continue or is it going to level out? More info. required.

Relatively new product. More info. required.

Life-cycle in apparent decline yet total market sales seem steady. What does this mean?

Projection

Containers

Projection

Cones

Toys

Water butts

Estimated total market take-up—water butts

Sales volume

Current sales

Time

1 year    2 years

**Figure A G3.1    Product audit: example of a completed life-cycle analysis**

166

# Action guide 4
# Creating a directional policy matrix

The directional policy matrix builds upon some of the ideas generated by the life-cycle analysis, but more importantly it enables one to assess which products or services or which groups of customers/segments will offer the best chance of commercial success. It will also aid decision-making about which products or services (or market segments) merit investment, both in terms of finance and managerial effort.

In this example, market segments are used. Although it is possible to use products or services, we recommend that you follow the instructions given below.

This is how you arrive at a directional policy matrix for your company.

1  List your market segments on a separate piece of paper and decide which ones are the most attractive. To arrive at these decisions you will no doubt take several factors into account including:

- the size of the markets
- their actual or prospective growth
- the prices you can charge
- profitability
- the diversity of needs (which you can meet)
- the amount of competition in terms of quality and quantity
- the supportiveness of the business environment
- technical developments,

Imagine that you have a measuring instrument, something like a thermometer, but which measures not temperature but market attractiveness. The higher the reading, the more attractive the market. This fabulous instrument is shown in Figure AG4.1.

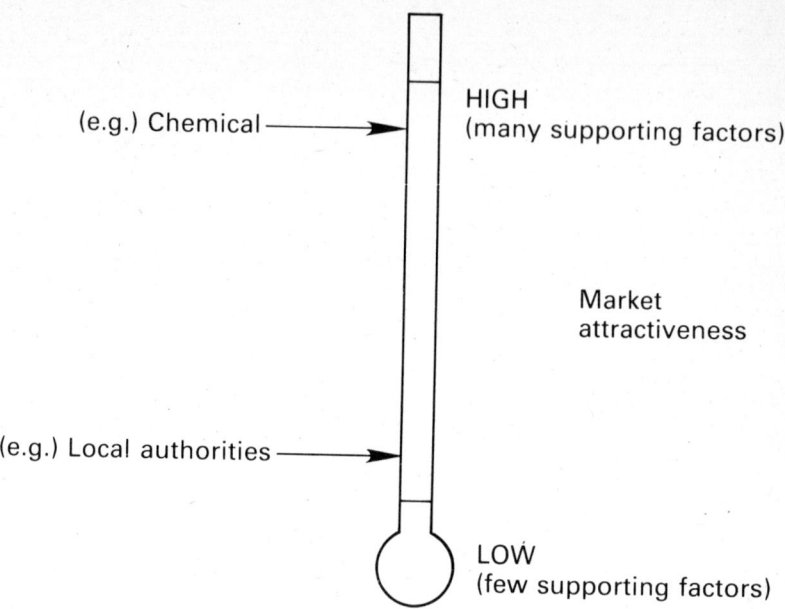

**Figure A G4.1   Market attractiveness thermometer**

Estimate the position on the scale each of your markets would record (should such an instrument exist) and make a note of it as shown by the figure.

2   Transpose this information on to Worksheet 4, writing in the markets, as shown in Figure AG4.2, on the left of the matrix.

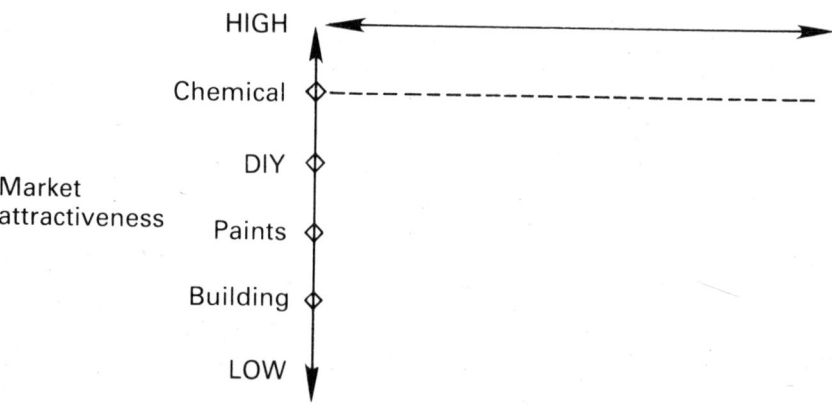

**Figure A G4.2   Ranking markets on the matrix**

3   Still using the worksheet, draw a dotted line horizontally across from the top left-hand market, as shown in Figure AG4.2.

4   Now ask yourself how well your company is equipped to deal with this most attractive market. A whole series of questions need to be asked to establish the company's business strengths, for example:

- Are we big enough?
- Can we grow?
- How large is our market share?
- Do we have the right products?
- How well are we known in this market?
- What image do we have?
- Do we have the right technical skills?
- Can we adapt to changes?
- Do we have funds to invest if required?
- Do we have enough capacity?
- How close are we to this market?
- How do we compare with competitors?

The outcome of such an analysis will enable you to arrive at a conclusion about the 'fitness' of your company, and you will be able to choose a point on the horizontal scale of the matrix to represent this. The left of this scale represents many company strengths; the right, few company strengths. Draw a vertical line from this point on the scale as shown in Figure AG4.3, so that it intersects with the horizontal line.

5   Repeat this process, estimating the company's business strengths, or capabilities to compete, in each of the markets you have listed on the left of the matrix. It is unlikely that the company will be equally strong in each market.

6   Now draw a circle around each intersection making the diameter of each circle proportional to that segment's share of your total sales turnover.

7   Now ask yourself the following questions:

- In which areas should you invest?
- Which product lines merit expansion or upgrading?
- Which products lend themselves to opportunistic development?
- In which markets should products be pruned?
- Which products ought to be eliminated?

If you need any help, refer to the completed example shown in

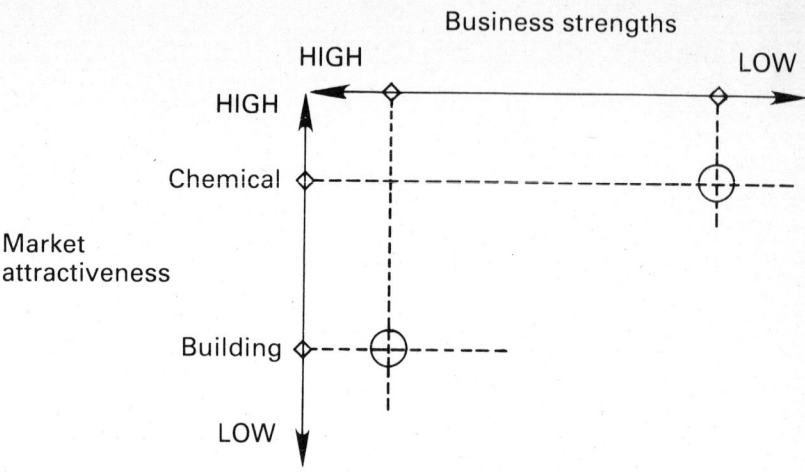

**Figure A G4.3   Representing business strengths on the matrix**

Figure AG4.4. It is, of course, possible to complete this exercise using products or services rather than market segments. If you do this, it will be necessary to change the vertical axis to read 'product/service attractiveness' (to you). Also, you will require different criteria.

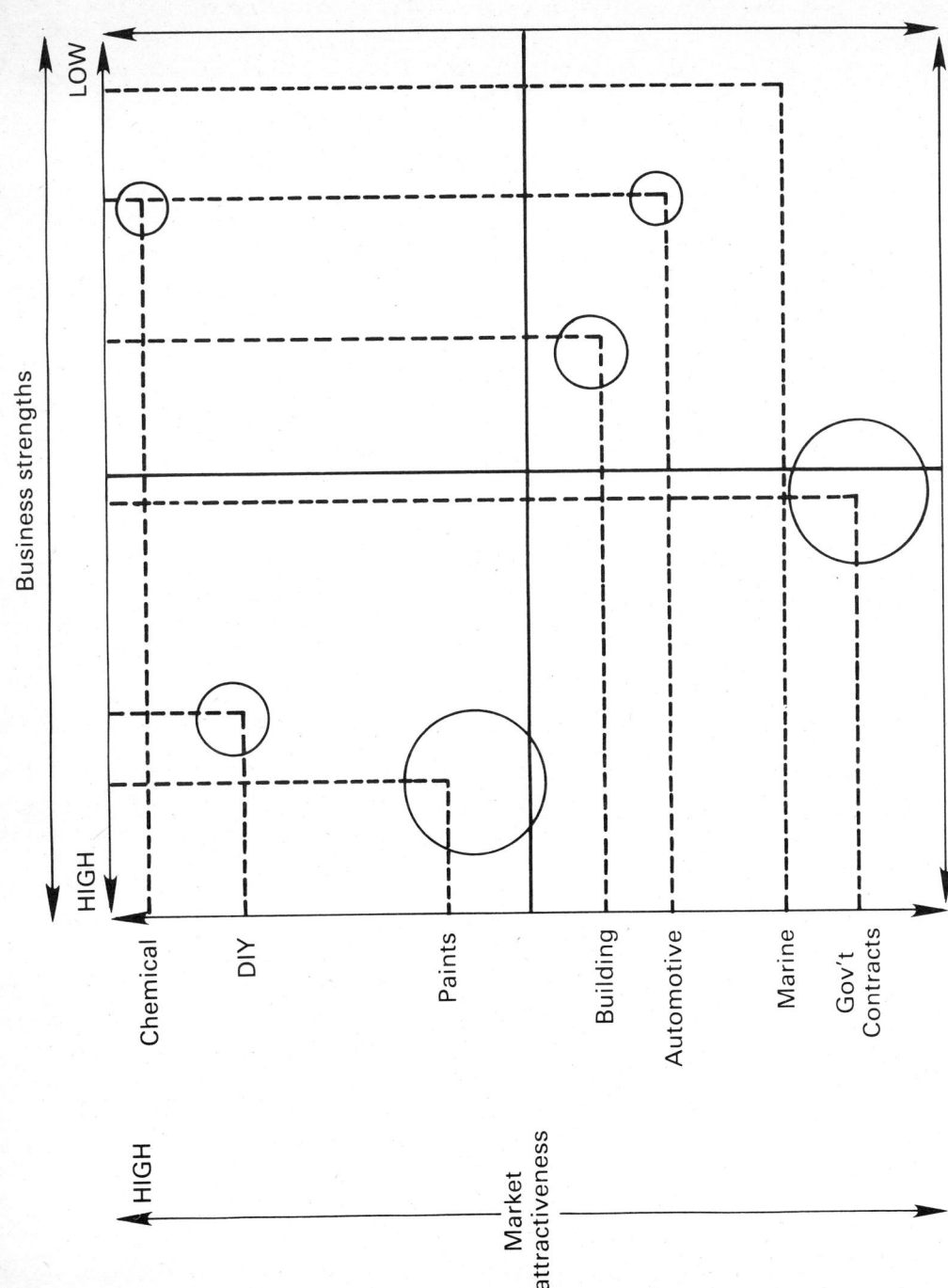

**Figure A G4.4  Example of a completed directional policy matrix**

**Worksheet 4   Directional policy matrix**

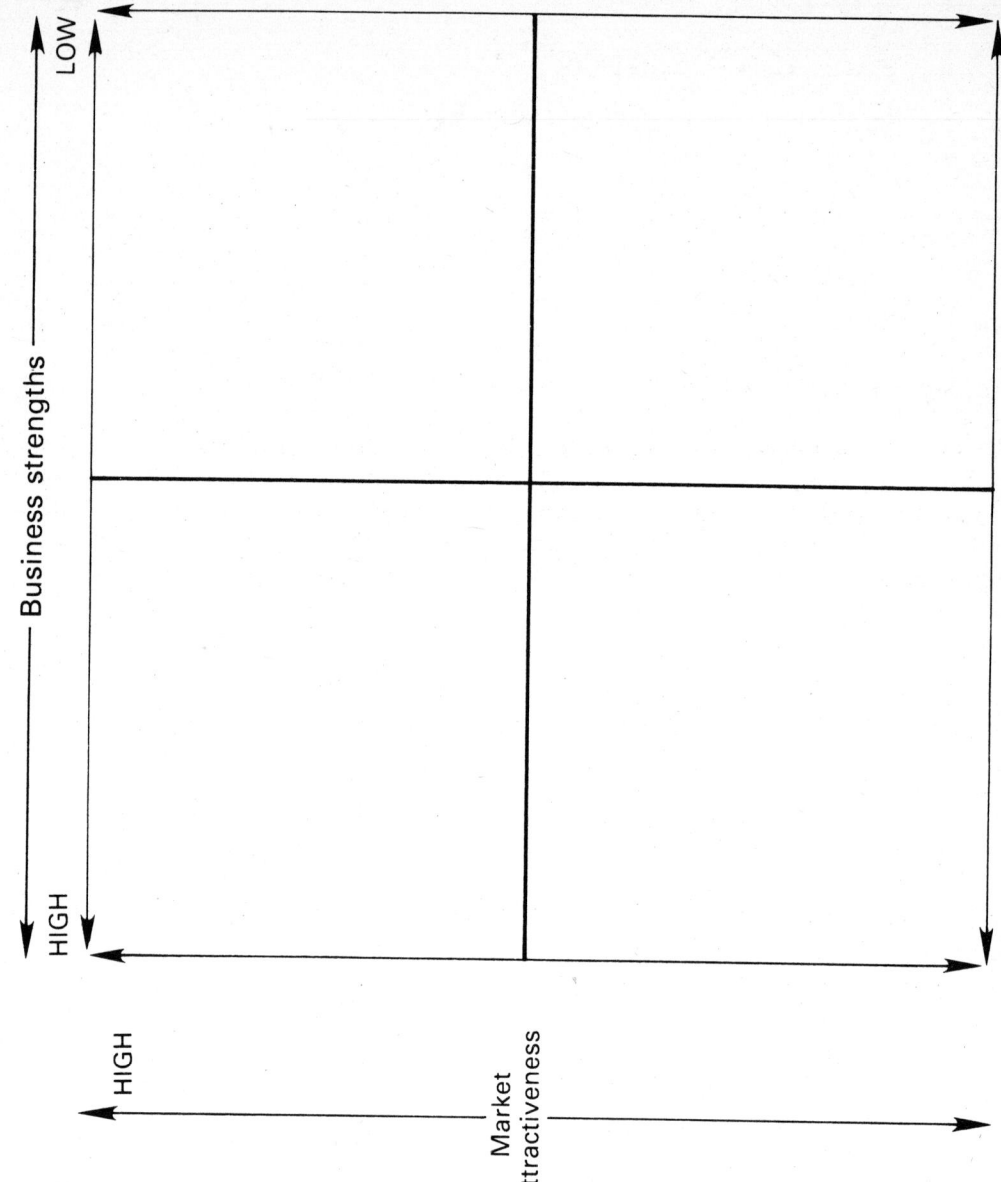

# Action guide 5
# Reviewing creativity

The creativity checklist which follows is designed to help you analyse how your organization uses the powerful tool of creative thinking. Answer the questions by scoring from low to high, with 1 being the lowest and 10 being the highest.

Which areas could be improved? Is there any specific action you can take to encourage creativity?

# CREATIVITY CHECKLIST

## General

| 1 | 2 | 3 | 4 | 5 | 6 | 7 | 8 | 9 | 10 |
|---|---|---|---|---|---|---|---|---|----|

- Is the firm's climate supportive of the generation and communication of ideas?

- Does top management take an interest in the whole idea-generation process (or does it simply expect to hear about ultimate successes)?

- Do people in the organization know who to address their ideas to?

- Is there a system for catching ideas before they get lost in an organizational bureaucracy?

- Does the firm undertake periodic 'idea generation' exercises in order:
    - to stimulate the climate for creativity, and
    - to generate ideas in order to solve problems and/or identify opportunities?

- Altogether, is management able to list the successful innovations that have been achieved during the previous few years? Has their number increased or declined?

## Information-gathering activities

- Has the company identified ways of collecting information which are cheaper and better than in the past?

- Does the marketing management monitor the cost–benefit of input collected during the year and seek to improve its pay-off value?

| | 1 | 2 | 3 | 4 | 5 | 6 | 7 | 8 | 9 | 10 |
|---|---|---|---|---|---|---|---|---|---|---|

- Does the company involve its distribution channels in the process of generating ideas and/or planning innovative strategies?

## Selling

- A sales force can be a fertile source of ideas. How effectively are such ideas tapped?

- Are members of the sales force ever invited to participate in idea-generation activities in response to non-marketing problems?

- Does the sales management try to identify what 'stars' of the sales force do which is different from the rest of the team?

- Is there a system for rewarding salesmen who produce ideas which are capable of being converted into successful innovations?

- Is there a procedure for cross-fertilizing ideas among the various regions/areas of the sales force?

## Promotion

- How many successful promotional examples can be listed in respect of the last few years and is the trend favourable?

- Has the cost–benefit of promotional campaigns improved?

- Do people inside the organization participate in the development of creative ideas to do with promotional activities or do they rely in the main on outside agencies to do the thinking for them?

- Does the company experiment with new communication techniques resulting from modern technologies?

- How effectively does the firm's management scan the commercial horizon to identify good ideas from other enterprises operating in the same field or in other fields?

## Distribution

- Has the company explored new ideas for distributing its products in order:
    - to cheapen the distribution process?
    - to make it more satisfying to the customers?

- Is the cost–benefit of the current logistics system being analysed at regular intervals?

- Does the marketing department reflect upon newer, better and cheaper methods of displaying its products at the 'point of sale' location?

- How successfully has the company managed to establish an interactive relationship with its customers and/or channels of distribution?

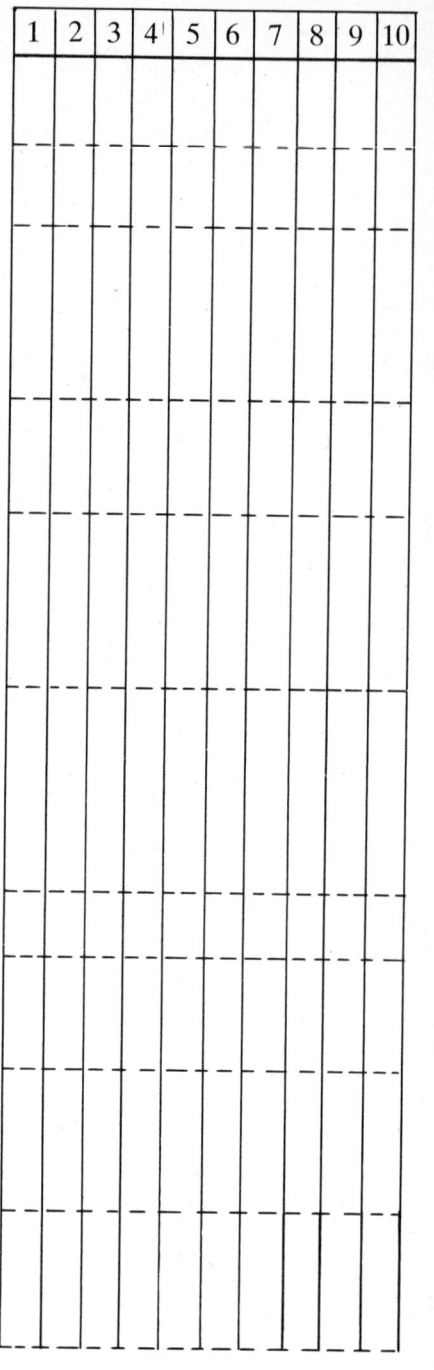

| 1 | 2 | 3 | 4 | 5 | 6 | 7 | 8 | 9 | 10 |
|---|---|---|---|---|---|---|---|---|----|

| 1 | 2 | 3 | 4 | 5 | 6 | 7 | 8 | 9 | 10 |
|---|---|---|---|---|---|---|---|---|---|

- Is there an attempt at comparing the relative cost of carrying out research activities with in-house personnel as against external resources?

## Product policy and planning

- What is the firm's record in the area of product development?

- How many product improvements and/or modifications have been successfully introduced?

- Has the rate of exchange between ideas and implementation improved?

## Pricing

- How many price ideas have been considered and how many of them have been implemented?

- Does the firm scan the outside environment in order to identify how different industries have managed to solve ticklish price problems?

- Does the company know how to manipulate its marketing strategies through creative pricing policies (e.g. use of experience curve analysis, price elasticity, pricing and positioning strategy, etc.)? Have a sufficient number of such examples taken place during the last few years and has the trend been favourable?

- Has the marketing team solved any pricing problems through non-price strategies?

# Select bibliography

Abell, D.F., *Defining the Business: The Starting Point of Strategic Planning*, Prentice Hall, 1980.

Abell, D.F. and Hammond, J.S., *Strategic Market Planning: Problems and Analytical Approaches*, Prentice Hall, 1979.

Buffa, E.S., *Meeting the Competitive Challenge*, Irwin, 1984.

James, B.G., *Business Wargames*, Abacus Press, 1984.

Kerin, R.A. and Peterson, R.A., *Perspectives on Strategic Marketing Management*, Allyn & Bacon, 1983.

Levitt, T., *The Marketing Imagination*, Free Press, 1983.

Ohmae, K., *The Mind of the Strategist*, Penguin Books, 1983.

Peters, T.J., and Waterman, R.H., *In Search of Excellence*, Harper & Row, 1982.

Porter, M.E., *Competitive Advantage: Creating and Sustaining Superior Performance*, Free Press, 1985.

Weitz, B.A. and Wensley, R., *Strategic Marketing: Planning, Implementation and Control*, Kent Publishing Co., 1984.

# Index